Mary H. Wills

A Winter in California

Mary H. Wills

A Winter in California

ISBN/EAN: 9783337251574

Printed in Europe, USA, Canada, Australia, Japan

Cover: Foto ©Andreas Hilbeck / pixelio.de

More available books at **www.hansebooks.com**

BY
MARY H. WILLS.

———

NORRISTOWN, PENNA.:
1889.

Entered, according to Act of Congress, in the year 1889, by
MARY H. WILLS,
In the Office of the Librarian of Congress at Washington.

MORGAN R. WILLS,
Printer and Publisher.

TO

MRS. ALAN WOOD, Jr.,

MY FRIEND AND FELLOW TRAVELER,
WITH WHOM THESE SCENES WERE ENJOYED,
I LOVINGLY DEDICATE THESE PAGES.

M. H. W.

PREFACE.

The chapters which compose this book were written in the idle moments of a Winter holiday. The scenes were new, the experiences pleasant, and the record a diversion.

Now that all has faded away, there comes, like the Alpen glow after sunset, a reflection of so much beauty and delight, that the mere recollection fills the heart with joy, and makes me long to live again amid the continual verdure of perpetual Summer.

Mrs. Mary H. Wills.

Norristown, Pa., 1889.

A WINTER IN CALIFORNIA.

I.

EN ROUTE.

To the Pacific Coast—Palaces on Wheels—People You Meet—Enchanting Scenery.

"Mary," said the editor without raising his admiring eyes from a fresh copy of the paper.

"Sire," replied a meek voice from the other side of the library table.

"Your throat improves but slowly; suppose you try the winter in Southern California."

"Your will is my pleasure," was the ready response. "Such a wise suggestion will receive my hearty co-operation and support."

And the sentence, which was preceded by a distressing cough, was punctuated by a most vicious hack.

"A woman whose vocal chords are impaired may in time lose her voice; and in that case her husband"—

That phrase is still incomplete. There was no further hint of masculine wisdom, for the answer, like one of Grant's campaigns, came "short, sharp and decisive," and without a suspicion of pulmonary punctuation. Then and there the matter was settled and the note of preparation sounded.

With this little allegorical prelude, modelled somewhat after a well-known Presidential fashion, we seem to need no further introduction or explanation to the reader.

In the notes which I hope to make during the coming months I will eschew the guide-book style —give neither heights, depths nor distances—write no word to enhance directly the price of a corner lot; but wave a free lance, and tell you of men, women and manners as I find them.

A Norristown party who returned in the early Autumn months gave enthusiastic accounts of the glories and wonders of this region. They climbed the mountain-side, explored canyons, followed dangerous trails, gazed on water-falls and monstrous trees, and were martyrs to the heat and dust in their pursuit of the grand and noble in nature. But I have come to sit in the glad sunshine, among the palm, fig and orange trees and flowers, and, viewing in calm content the landscape o'er, drink in great draughts of health and vigor. Then, should hope and anticipation be realized, when Spring comes, light-footed and laden with sweet perfumes, I too will climb mountains, explore caves, and learn new lessons of God's handiwork as unfolded in the book of Nature.

Mrs. Mary A. Livermore, the foremost American woman thinker of the present day, says there are two forms of the genus tramp. The one a homeless vagabond, who besieges your back door two hours after meal-time in his search for hot coffee, and finding it not waxes wroth, then with imploring voice, ragged garments, and a general air of good-for-nothingness, beseeches further charity. The other, a class, who, enjoying what Matthew Arnold calls "beastly prosperity," have homes in which they do not like to stay, but go wandering over the world in quest of pleasure and information. Both suffer because they are not rooted in homes, which, never "so humble," or never so grand, give an anchorage to the human being. Now I confess to a little of the tramp instinct—to a desire to go out into the world, see its workings, and, reflecting thereon, make my own deductions.

If a person is able to travel in a first-class manner none need hesitate to undertake this long journey of three thousand miles. Modern railroading has become reduced to such a science that both comforts and luxuries are provided. We are all familiar with the speed and safety of the main artery which traverses our great Keystone Commonwealth and adjacent states, and lands you quickly in Chicago, at which place a sleeper may be procured, and there is no further change until your destination is reached. At various points most excellent eating-houses are found, all under one management, and a first-class meal awaits you with plenty of time to enjoy it. When I saw announced that the handsomest train of cars in the world was to be found on this division, I smiled and, to draw it mildly, called it Western enthusiasm. When I saw them I smiled again, but it was at my own folly, for surely no palace on wheels was ever before so beautified. The carpets are the richest texture and most serviceable patterns; draperies of Gobelin blue with fringes and tassels of the latest and most unique styles; mirrors of bevelled glass, plate glass windows, handsome wood carvings, delicate frescoes, electric lights and steam-heating apparatus. Can modern civilization do more?

Many of these things are entirely out of keeping with those who use them. Children, I suppose, have their rights, one of which is to travel when accompanied by parents, but I submit that it is vandalism for even these darlings to climb over such seats, drink milk at their pleasure, and flourish cold chicken's legs in such places. As well might you feed them at home in the parlor. I remember the story which is old but good, of the long-suffering visitor who had been annoyed by the undue prominence given at dinner to a precocious child, and when asked for a toast, drained his glass to the "memory of the much-abused Herod."

The first day's journey is apt to be unsatisfactory. People are stiff, have not lost the home feeling, nor begun to fraternize, but as time rolls on, with one common destination they rapidly become acquainted, visit each other, play various games, compare ideas, and have a real good, jolly time. One morning, when, several hours late, the want of breakfast was openly discussed, one lady, the proud possessor of a coffee-pot, brewed a "jorum" of tea, and all sat with thankful hearts, applauded her skill, and drank to fill an aching void.

There is generally much to interest an aggregation of people. This occasion was no exception. One party of Eastern people were conveying a wife and mother to San Diego, hoping in that mild yet bracing climate to win health to a frame wasted to the last extremity by consumption. I never saw such devoted attention as she had. They deadened her sensibilities with opiates, then exhilarated her with whiskey and champagne, and finally stimulated her with effervescing compounds. They were evidently not followers of the doctrine of Christian science, the first and cardinal principle of which is to keep the mind from self, for they ministered to her constantly. Paradoxical as it may seem, the husband was a Congregationalist minister, a fact I never would have suspected when I saw him play a skillful game of cards, smoke, and handle the corkscrew with the air of an expert. He was in demand as a story-teller, and told many good ones. Yet I failed to discover in them an exhortation or an epistle. He belonged to the school of muscular

Christianity, and was interested in deer-hunting, trout-fishing, and camp-life generally. I could not see that he lacked in the Christian graces. He only added others, and certainly the devotion he manifested to a sick and not very attractive partner would overbalance many shortcomings. It always causes a thrill of sadness to see any one "far from home and all its pleasures," when we know that the end is surely drawing nigh.

I remember in my youth being particularly impressed with the sad story of a lad, who, possessing what was as rare in those days as now, started out with a determination to win a name and fortune for himself and make a home for the declining years of two unsuccessful parents. How brightly the battle of life opened, and how assiduously he labored for a few years. Then strength failed and the physician said he must leave the crowded city and confinement of a banking-house, and go down among the pines of New Jersey, and by open-air exercise and great care he might win back the bloom and vigor of manhood. For a time the charm worked, then failed, and the physician said go to Denver, for in that pure, dry air miracles are effected. Then he dragged his poor, weak form miles from those who loved him best, and his new-found friends, seeing the end was nigh, sent for the anxious, watching mother, who daily expected the summons. On she came as fast as steam could bring her, and, meeting with neither delay nor accident, like the Spartan mother that she was, approached with a smiling face the bedside of her dying boy. Who can tell what endearments passed between them, what tender confidences were exchanged, and in broken phrases what kindly inquiries made for those at home? Then, when the half had not been told, they lay quietly down side by side to sleep. Silently the weary watchers stole from the room and patiently waited their recall. Hours slipped by. Impatience and fear took the place of hope, and with no word they went in. Sleep had been kindly to the mother, and fatigue and suffering had been replaced by a peaceful calm; but her boy's face was glorified, for the angel of death had been there and he was awake to joy in Paradise.

Enough of gloom and sad forebodings. Let me tell you of the weather. While your coast was devastated by snow, rain and heavy gales, we travelers experienced naught but warmth and sunshine. Chicago gave us a biting welcome, and the breeze from the lake was fresh and sharp; so we bade her adieu. In Kansas our two weeks were composed of bright, warm, sunshiny days, clear, starlit nights, and an atmosphere dry, mild and pleasant. The presence of countless turkeys told of the approach of Thanksgiving, but really we felt it might be May. I never saw such sunsets as Kansas produces. There is nothing to distract, and the eye can sweep the whole horizon, as it were, and see the most beautiful tints of blue, orange, pink and gold melt away and gradually be swallowed up in the gloom of night.

For picturesque beauty our route, except in occasional places, is in no way remarkable. It is direct and safest at this season to avoid snow. In Kansas you pass vast ranches and see immense herds of poor-looking cattle; in New Mexico you ride through the wide green meadows called "vegas"; and in Arizona pine forests, deserts and rocky formations meet the eye. On both sides the track these bold boulders loom up mountain high, while above and overshadowing all are the different mountain ranges covered with the eternal snow.

The character of vegetation changes with the latitude. In the desert we see none at all; then growing in rocky beds, with nothing apparently to fertilize, we find immense cacti, Spanish daggers, yuccas by the millions, cedars covered with little blue berries, mistletoe, and unproductive sage brush. The vastness of these great patches of sterility makes the eyes ache, everything is so wide and great. No wonder Dr. Hall, failing to receive the expected call, went home disgusted with such an expanse of country, and complained that he was fatigued on reaching different prominent points. John Bull, when he comes to lecture in New York, visit Niagara, Washington, and to cross the Rocky Mountains, during his six weeks' vacation, finds he has a very large contract on hand, and necessarily spends much of the time in a sleeper.

A description of this section of our country would scarce be considered complete without some reference to its aboriginal inhabitants, who, looking like very tame, dirty Indians, swarm around the stations and either beg or try to dispose of their nondescript wares and shrivelled apples. I warn any one who has an admiration for the noble red man and his handsome squaw not to take this trip, under fear of disenchantment. Dirty beyond description, with hair unkempt, wearing rags for garments, but always wrapped in a filthy blanket, they are not pleasing to look upon. Some of the children are nearly naked; and, as some one wickedly remarked, if the boys had a garment it was the Seymour pattern and shape. The men have sullen countenances, and seem quarrelsome in disposition, while the women have lost the traits and charms of femininity, and many look like idiots.

Days and nights of unceasing travel roll by and nature gives sign that the end of our journey is nigh. The grass becomes green, the beautiful and graceful pepper tree with crimson-laden boughs becomes more abundant. Eucalyptus, live-oak and cottonwood show their sturdy trunks, and last come fig, olive and orange, laden with bud, blossom and golden fruit.

The journey is over; we have reached the portals of the Golden Gate, and Pasadena, fitly termed the "Crown of the Valley," is our resting place.

Surely He who created all nature must have pronounced this very good, for Eden was not fairer. As far as the eye can reach the great mountain ranges of Sierra Madre and San Bernardino stretch out their arms and let the sunlight and the shadows play upon them. High above all, with hoary head covered with the snows of a thousand years, towers

Old Baldy, a sentinel by day and a watch by night, and in the lovely valley thus formed we gather the flowers and fruits beloved by mankind. Perched upon an eminence, embosomed in a forest of plants and vines, sits "The Raymond."

It is an enchanting scene, far surpassing description, and for the moment I am blind to its beauties. Like Puck, I'll "put a girdle round the earth," and in thought am with you where skies are leaden, winds whistling, and sleet and rain falling, but where a loving heart is anxiously watching and waiting for the electric spark to tell of our safety and well-doing. The illusion lasts but a moment, and I awake to see a sky as blue as Italy, a day as perfect as June, and a loveliness so new and rare that both tongue and pen must falter to tell of it. Masses of roses greet me on every side. The rooms are redolent with their rich perfume, and a hundred plants of which I have yet to tell send incense to the skies.

Enough for one time. I came from you, dear friends, in quest of that great boon, health. The malady from which I suffer has not dimmed the eye nor dulled my powers of imagination. You gave me a wealth of good wishes, such as makes me humble when I recall them. Advice, always an abundant commodity, was freely showered upon me. Some scoffed that I should go so far to obtain that which with care and prudence was within my reach at home. To such I turned a deaf ear. Others, and by far the largest class, bade me God-speed. To these I listened. Sometimes I think with Shakspeare's famous traveler, "when I was at home I was in a better place, but travelers must be content."

And now let me ask of you, one and all, in the language of the gay and insouciant Steerforth, when he went out from home and friends, "to think of me at my best," and I know I will be content.

II.

THEN AND NOW.

The Climate—Greed for Gain—The Typical Land Agent—John Brown's Sons—Flower and Fruit.

THERE is no place where you are so busy being idle as when you go from home and have nothing to do. The divisions of time being different, methods of amusement so varied, days glide into weeks without a seeming succession of time. When you leave home in the summer you leave comfort and the conveniences of life behind with "dull care." You say you escape the heat, knowing that to be a pleasant fiction; but the one who is so fortunate as to exchange the chilling and biting frosts of our Eastern winter for the mild, equable climate of Southern California, may indeed be congratulated. We may have forethought, but we have not as much sense as the bird. One whir, and he is off to seek food and shelter in the land of fruit and sunshine.

To talk with the inhabitants, be they old or recent converts, not Paradise itself can surpass in delights this now famous region. In dryness they insist that it is superior to the much-vaunted south of France and Italy, more nearly in winter resembling the climate of Egypt, where the heat is never excessive nor of an enervating character. As we have seen it we should say it was not warm enough to be likened to a summer day nor so cool as to be compared to our spring weather. At home we have no type which exactly fits it. You can walk at midday without fatigue, and let the sun pour upon you without discomfort. This remarkable climate, the virtues of which are of ancient date, seems rather a recent discovery. The Argonauts of '49 neither saw nor told of it. Their greed was for

> "Gold! gold! gold! gold!
> Bright and yellow, hard and cold,"

and forsaking home comforts they undertook the then arduous journey of months across the plains— left behind them the refinements of civilization to which they had been accustomed, and joining the lawless hordes here gathered sought in the bowels of the earth for that which glitters. The discouragements they met, the disasters which followed, history and romance now tell. Broken-hearted and despondent wrecks of manhood, many came back poor in purse, morally and socially ruined, with only words of wisdom to warn others of the snares and pit-falls into which they had fallen. Judge Lynch and the Vigilance Committee were the law; murder, arson and robbery passed unrebuked, and crimes at which humanity might blush were condoned and the perpetrators allowed to go unmolested. Human life was held at low value, and a man was as likely to be shot at his fire-side as in the miners' camp.

Now that the whole country has become a sanitarium, as it were, an invalid must exercise the same caution as at home. Even the much-vaunted climate will work no miracle. It will, under certain conditions, assist nature. The evenings are remarkably cool, and you must not expose yourself to the night air until you become acclimated. In fact, you must do nothing to excess or you will pay the penalty. A light wood or soft coal fire will be found to diffuse a most grateful heat.

The real prosperity of California has not yet begun. A vast territory, with unequaled advantages, a few far-seeing capitalists not many years ago started a "boom." Forthwith people emigrated by thousands. Competing railways rivaled each other in the low fares they advertised. Those here left their peaceful industries and daily avocations, and in their haste to be rich took their available funds and bought up and divided thousands of acres into sections and town lots, driving their stakes throughout the wilderness and even up the mountain side. It is the old story of covetousness, its tardy recognition and subsequent punishment, for the land did not become worth its weight in gold as they fondly imagined it would, but is left upon their hands, with taxes accumulating, still untilled; and they who saw in themselves prospective Mackays, Floods and Crockers, will be forced to part with their possessions. When owned and cultivated by honest, horny-handed sons of toil, the real prosperity of California will be established.

There are in this locality miles of the finest asphalt pavement, the putting down of which is expensive and we well know increases taxation. In many places it runs through bare and uncultivated sections, and is allowed to remain covered with sand and an accumulation of dirt. We, whose eyes are accustomed to cleanliness of sidewalk, are quick to note and appreciate these defects.

In the laying out of streets beautiful orange groves in full bearing have been sacrificed, and anything and everything ruthlessly destroyed in what was thought to be the march of public improvement.

In Pasadena stores doing a moderate trade bring an annual rental of twelve hundred dollars. Last year twenty-four hundred was asked and obtained without difficulty for the same property. It is very easy to obtain information in this region, for the representative New Englander is here in full force, and with the characteristic "I want to know" never hesitates to ask a question.

The country is overstocked with physicians, lawyers and men who have come out here to earn a living by their wits; and, if we mistake not, unless they go resolutely to work to gain bread in the old-fashioned and unpopular "sweat of the brow" manner, some will be reduced to dire straits.

En route I met an elderly man, who, from his varied stock of intelligence, some of it really valuable, and his extreme volubility, I judged to be a land agent. One of the great recommendations which everything seemed to possess in his eyes was that it was so new, and the highest compliment which he could pay a town or village was the fact that a couple of years back it had neither "local habitation nor name." Finally wearied with his incessant chatter, and desiring to use my eyes as my own judge, I said, "It is no recommendation to Eastern people to find everything so new. The rage now with us is for the old, and the more antique, from family to furniture, the more valuable we esteem it." He paused for an instant, and then rejoined in the most undaunted manner: "Madam, you go to San Jose, one of the first settled towns; many of the houses are crumbling; the roses grow like grape-vines. There you will find things sufficiently ancient to please you." They always try to suit you. If the oranges are sour, they explain that the season of ripeness is not yet come. If the grapes are dry, they are intended for raisin culture. The wine lacks flavor only because of recent vintage. Everything will be right, provided always we hit the proper time.

Pasadena boasts of fourteen churches, and claims that they are totally incapable of holding the throngs of people who worship in them. The Presbyterian denomination have erected in the past two years a beautiful edifice. It is built in the style of an amphitheatre, provided with a first-class organ, artistic stained glass windows, ornately frescoed walls and ceiling, and aisles neatly carpeted in the best style.

The pulpit on the Sabbath was a bower of loveliness, for the graceful boughs of the pepper tree were entwined with roses, ferns, heliotrope and lilies, all which dispensed a sweet-smelling incense to the skies. I deeply thought as I sat so many miles from the accustomed place, and saw no familiar face, but listened to the old, old story, which, wherever heard, is the same strain of the Heavenly Father, His mercy and His love.

Since "westward the course of empire takes its way," we thought to find the country, broad as it is, somewhat crowded; but you can walk on the highways and byways for many miles and meet no human being. I remember a dozen years ago, when preparing to go to Europe, I talked with an old friend in regard to the dangers of the sea voyage. Shaking his grey head sagaciously, he said: "Too many people go nowadays, for my taste; the ocean, wide as is her pathway, is too full for me to risk my life upon it." When six days out and hungering for the sight of humanity our eyes for the first time were gladdened by a strange craft, my old friend's words recurred to me, and I thought the sea was not crowded on her bosom.

The whole town is traversed and environed with street cars, which from lack of patronage run at irregular and inconvenient intervals. Comparatively speaking, there seems to be as much track, in a direct ratio to the size of the place, as New York requires for her restless thousands of people. Old jokes with regard to the "air line," and the loneliness of horse and driver, have reached here, and are revived and enjoyed. Some of the lines confess that they run at a loss of twenty dollars per day. Still this is not an exceptional case nor peculiar to a benighted region, for well do I know a large and civilized town, three thousand miles from here, where the directors are all men of sagacity and intelligence, yet in the face of opposition they built and equipped a road, now run it, losing money daily, and do not expect a dividend until the millenium.

Upon the side of the Sierra Madre, near a large canyon, but within easy driving distance, live two sons of John Brown, he of soul-marching memory. They have a great, barren, uncultivated farm, which, of course, they dignify by the title of ranch. The houses they have built themselves we would scarce deem habitable; but they appear content, and are hale, hearty, stalwart and happy. The great problem of human liberty which caused their father to lay down his life seems to find no echo in their breasts; they are about as plain, common-place men as you would meet. Like some of our business firms, if they gain fame it will be as their "father's sons." One of them tells the story of his domestic life without any hint of infelicity, and explains his loneliness by saying, "My wife does not like it here, so she always lives in Ohio," evidently thinking the contract to be a pliable one, and that no constraint should be used to compel a woman to live where she does not want to. I wonder whether he could answer the oft quoted "Is marriage a failure?"

I firmly believe that the climate of this state contains all the virtues claimed for it. Nowhere are the skies so blue, the sun so bright, and the foliage and flowers so perfect as here. Yet people see things so differently at the same time and place, that scarcely any of the information you receive can be relied upon. We were told that at this season we would be likely to encounter much rain and dampness. Forthwith an outfit of umbrellas, "galoches and mackintoshes" were procured; yet we have been absent a month, and to-day saw the first drop of rain. Then, again, they said, Take winter clothing. So we equipped with warm, stout garments and wraps. Behold! the days are like May, and we sigh for straw hats and parasols.

A lady in Atchison said, "You know the flowers in California are mammoth in size, but it is at the expense of their perfume." That was a disappointment; but we took it with a "grain of salt," grasped the first rose we saw after leaving the train, buried our face in its dewy petals, and, behold! the odors of "Araby the blest" were not more spicy. Every one should come twice, I deduce, and on the second trip they will know what to expect and what is required.

And now a few words in relation to the flowers, with which I each day hold converse sweet. They are incomparable. Around and about the pillars of the porch whereon I love to sit, there twines in graceful luxuriance a passion vine, whose flowers of brilliant red are to me new and strange. It is unlike any we have, but bears the same similitude to the "cross and passion" as its purple sister, with which we are acquainted. In the beds are rows of all varieties: heliotrope and lantanas grown to the size of dwarf pear trees, lilies, oxalis so evergrown that I did not recognize an old friend, poinsettias in brilliant and gaudy scarlet dress, abutilons grown to the size of an ordinary lilac bush, coleus, geraniums, ferns, palms, the cacti of sub-tropical regions, beside decorative plants in great variety. In a word, the *tout ensemble* is bloom, beauty and perfume.

Of the fruits of this valley we can say but little. This is not the proper season for testing their virtues. Yet as an earnest of what may yet come, everywhere the landscape is dotted with vineyards and orchards, and we see lemon, lime, olive, peach, apple, apricot, plum, pear, guava, pomegranate, Japanese persimmon, banana, and other fruit trees.

One thing which serves to beautify the landscape is the absence of fences. A simple hedge of cypress, more or less ornamental, serves as the dividing line. I think the residents must have been extremely annoyed by the depredations of visitors, for never have I seen such numerous warnings and penalties as here in regard to trespassing. The female character seems to be thoroughly understood, for while in most groves you are permitted to gather such oranges as you may want there are the most stringent regulations in regard to culling a single rose, showing that they deem woman's desire for adornment a far greater passion than her appetite.

An orange grove, with dark green leaves, delicate white blossoms and golden fruit, is beautiful in the distance. On near approach the plowed soil, so necessary to its well-doing, and the absence of green sward, presents an unsightly appearance. The want of beautiful lawn-grass is likewise a disappointment. True, hills and valleys are with "verdure clad," but it is a small green vine or moss which covers them, not the modest clover whose emerald hues we know so well and love.

Far be it for me to decry one trait in what some pronounce so nearly perfect that they deem this the last, best work of the Creator and pronounced by him very good. This is a great but growing country; in infancy as regards cultivation. The conditions are the most favorable. She *will* be a giant among states, and nations yet unborn will see and rejoice in her prosperity. Every advancement of science is here welcomed and in active use. In intelligence, in art, and literature, they are fully equal to their fellow-men. In wonderful stories, in exaggerated ideas, in great, glorious, marvellous achievements, they surpass the world. I think John Chinaman's idea of things the correct one. When asked to invest some of his hard-earned hoard in town-lots he shook his head sagaciously, winked his eyes knowingly, and said in a mild-mannered way, "Me no do it; too much bye and bye." So it is. California's greatness is for the future.

III.

PASADENA.

Christmas Time Without Christmas Weather—Personal Mention—The Raymond Excursions.

CHRISTMAS and cold weather are as indissolubly connected as fire-works and Fourth of July, and it is in opposition to all preconceived ideas to buy fir trees when wearing straw hats and seeking the friendly shade of a parasol. Reindeers and sleighs do not have the same significance when seen in a temperature of 70°, and we doubt whether even here old Santa Claus is as warmly welcomed as in the regions of ice and snow. Yet the dear old holiday time, if it has any significance, religious or social, should not be a thing of latitude or longitude. It is universal, and the glad cry, " Peace on earth, good will to men," should resound o'er all the civilized world.

Startling as the reality, we can scarce believe the near approach of Christmas. We miss the shops with their increased and alluring stores of beautiful goods; the travelers overloaded with bundles; the cheerful greetings among the high and low; the great outpouring of humanity, who, despite rain, hail and nipping frost, are by day and night in search of Christmas goods. We wonder if the little boys and girls on the Pacific slope are deceived and mystified by the pleasing picture of old Santa Claus, and whether they dance as merrily as some we wot of in anticipation of the opening of his pack. Let us hope that the good old festival time, when all gather around the family hearth-stone, is still a joyous and happy one, and that amid all pleasures and merriment the absent are not forgotten.

Los Angeles, to which we paid our first visit, aspires to be second in numbers and importance in the rank of cities in the state. Like all places which have suddenly sprung into existence, it is a conglomeration of races. Long-haired Mexicans, almond-eyed Chinese, sturdy Germans, Irish and Spaniards jostle each other in the streets, and commingle tongues with a strange and startling effect. The best dwellings, many of them pretentious in style, are built upon the brow of the overhanging hills, and access to their locality by cable car is both prompt and cheap. Many of the houses are built of wood, but one story high, and generally surrounded by flourishing gardens or lawns. In the business portion of the city they have patterned after foreign lands, and the "Louvre," the "City of Paris," and strange unpronounceable Chinese and Japanse names are conspicuously displayed.

The streets are filled with what may well be denominated a rabble of idle, dissolute men. The trademarks of civilization, in the shape of liquor-saloons, pool-rooms and dens of untold iniquity, are seen on every side, and vice openly flaunts itself in the face of passers-by. Many buildings are in course of erection, and the attendant mortar-beds, guy-ropes, derricks for hoisting stone and brick, all combine to render the sidewalks undesirable places for promenading. In fact, I saw nothing to attract or interest save for a day. The California women, respectable matrons and maids I mean, are entirely too free with cosmetics to suit a sober taste. Not alone do they attempt to repair the ravages of time, but young girls, on whose faces should be naught but the bloom of youth, resort to the same means. I will say, however, they are very honest about it, putting both powder and paint on in such quantities that concealment is not to be thought of, and then further disfiguring themselves by pencilled eye-brows and bleached hair.

Any one familiar with the geography of our country would, without much thought, know that the winter season is not the proper time to either see or enjoy the fruits of this section. You would, however, suppose that a reasonable amount of care would be exercised in regard to their preservation. Millions of pounds, for lack of transportation, decay annually; yet I verily believe there are more and better grapes in and around Broad street station than you will find exposed for sale in any portion of Southern California. Here is an industry of untold wealth. The purchase and consumption of fruit is so universal that in this country, now a Mecca to pilgrims, some means for its preservation should be devised. Strawberries of rather doubtful quality can now be obtained, green peas, corn, beets, cauliflower and squashes are abundant, and the writer partook of a very good watermelon plucked from a garden on the mountain side.

The rides and drives about Pasadena form the chief entertainment for its visitors. The air is pure, the sun's rays sufficiently warm, the roads as hard as though macadamized, and many of them, shaded by eucalyptus and pepper trees, wind through orange and lemon groves. The innocence of the modern female travelers was never more apparent than when I heard them commenting on the great but recent growth of these giants which were overhanging us, never exercising thought, or the suggestion, that these monarchs of the primeval forests had been left standing, and were not, as they supposed, the result of a score of years.

The wine-making interests of California are vast in extent, and a visit to what are known as the Sunny Slope vineyards of San Gabriel, owned and operated by L. J. Rose & Co., will serve to pass a pleasant morning. There is of course but little of the actual process to be seen at this season. The vines are brown and bare. No grapes are received after September 18th, but the *modus operandi* can be inspected and the fruits of the vintage tested. What huge vats and tanks are employed in this business! What capital involved, and what profits realized! It makes one shudder to think of it. Both American and Chinese laborers are employed, and much skill, care and cleanliness are exercised in every detail. The annual product of the house they estimate at four hundred thousand gallons, consisting principally of brandy, port, sherry, angelica, claret and light table wines. No champagne is made. No wine leaves the cellar under one year, and some, which requires age to mellow it, is held for fourteen. The proprietors claim that the peculiar sweet quality of these grapes, ripened by an almost tropical sun, renders them particularly adapted for the manufacture of this enemy, which men put into their mouths to steal away their brains, and which Shakespeare characterizes as "O thou invisible spirit of wine, if thou hast no name to be known by, let us call thee devil."

And now, my little temperance lecture ended, let us push a few miles further, and close to the Sierra Madre Mountains we reach the ranch of E. J. Baldwin, or, as he is familiarly known, "Lucky Baldwin," a man who owns sixty-five thousand acres of land, and

>"Whose cattle are grazing,
>Their heads never raising,
>There are forty feeding like one."

This gentleman seems to combine the old proverb, and to be both lucky and rich. It is said that his horses always win the races; that his hounds are in at the death; and that his three wives have been divorced, each with an alimony of seventy-five thousand dollars. In things temporal this modern Bluebeard may have been successful, but his domestic affairs must be in a great muddle. Let us resort to Scripture, for surely "He heapeth up riches, and knoweth not who shall gather them." He has lakes and fish-ponds, orange-groves and flower-gardens, stables, stores, vineyards, and mansions, but over all there hangs an air of neglect not pleasant to see in a land where the advantages of nature can be so easily supplemented by man's labor and made to be fruitful.

Unlike Florida, the soil here needs no fertilizers. Turn it up with the plow, irrigate it, and the harvest will be plenteous.

One characteristic of this place is certainly peculiar, and deserves to be chronicled. We all have read and ridiculed the uncommon neatness of the matrons of Holland, who require both guest and family to leave their shoes outside the door, lest they carry dust or dirt into the house. Here, outside of almost every front door, hangs a feather dusting-brush, and every one who approaches is expected to test its merits upon his shoes ere he crosses the threshold. Ignorance, and not impoliteness, has hitherto prevented our adopting this most cleanly but uncommon practice.

We have with us a literary celebrity, one whose name was a household word to the readers of fiction a score of years ago—Miss Virginia F. Townsend—a woman of ability, whose pen has given us much that was good and pure in the realms of romance. Personally she is not attractive. Her most ardent admirer, her warmest friend, would acknowledge her plain; but her face is kindly, her voice low and trainante, and from her lips you hear no word save for the good of man and womankind. It is hard to think that the pen-children of this most commonplace old maid should be such miracles of loveliness; that she, who evidently was never won, should know how to woo in dulcet tones; and that the hand which always portrays the beauty and charm of domestic life should write itself a wanderer. The world is full of contradictions. The author of "Home, Sweet Home," was an exile, with no place to lay his head.

Miss Townsend has come here not to enjoy rest, but for change and to do some literary work. She confesses that her task is a hard one; she cannot shut out the beauties of hill and dale and devote herself to pen and paper. In the grandeur and richness of her surroundings her enthusiastic and emotional nature is aroused. She confesses that, although a careful reader, she is amazed and charmed by the unexpected luxuriousness of out-door growth and natural scenery.

I was asked before leaving home to look closely into the workings of the Raymond excursions, and give some that were halting the benefit of my inquiry. Ample means have been at my disposal to examine the system, and I most unhesitatingly give it my humble approval. Newspaper people are rarely accused of being disinterested, but before going into details let me say that I was not a member of an excursion, nor under any obligations to praise it. For the benefit and enlightenment of many who desire to travel, but who are prevented doing so by lack of suitable company, I would say place yourself under charge of the party by all means. First, you will be spared all trouble as regards tickets, meals, baggage, sleepers, and other necessary and prolific sources of dissension. The conductor attends faithfully to all these charges, and stands between you and imposition. The special points of the journey are shown you, and, if deemed advisable, visited. You will go in first-class style, and a little cheaper than you can travel alone. Now I do not mean that the very worthy gentlemen who are the pioneers in this business are philanthropists, or conduct it for love. They make money, but they have reduced it to such a system that they are enabled to do so. Rates of travel here are much higher than with us; accommodations infinitely poorer. *They* take advantage of round-trip or excursion fares, own controlling interests in large hotels, send their own shrewd, sharp Yankee conductors in advance to make bargains, and can by their fiat make or unmake a resort. In a word, they have made themselves a business of such magnitude that the people dare not disregard them, but are anxious to conciliate these interests. The dignified New York *Tribune*, in a recent issue, thus sneers at the modern traveler, and says: "California is happy because the Eastern tender-foot is again in the land, scattering shekels in his customary Eastern way." Raymond and Whitcomb will protect the innocent stranger, and see that none of the shekels are diverted.

Regularity of meals is always conducive to the health and good temper of the inner man, and, as a local celebrity says, "consequently woman." Let me instance. In no section of country will be found better eating-houses than along the Santa Fe route. They are all models of cleanliness and promptness, with food in great variety, excellently cooked, and served in a model manner. But frequently trains are hours behind time, and, with a desert before you, it sometimes happens that there is no breakfast until noon, no supper until midnight. Raymond has his own dining-car, and whether in a mountain or a morass, the meal is always forthcoming at the proper time. Of course every one cannot have the middle berth on the popular side in the sleeper, but I believe as far as possible succession in application procures impartial accommodations. Everything is set forth in the itinerary, and they fulfill every promise, not one whit more nor one jot less. If they set down a carriage ride you will be given it, neither crowded within nor without. I have talked much with those around me during the past month, and there has been no word of broken faith. I met one old lady who complained that "The Raymond" was not situated in the valley, utterly oblivious to the fact that its picturesque elevation and magnificent view of the adjacent country gives it one of the finest sweeps of landscape in the world.

Never have I witnessed a scene of such regal beauty as a few nights ago when returning from a walk I was attracted by the extreme and marked loveliness of the western horizon. The whole sky was a mass of crimson and gold, flecked with clouds, which deepened into violet and a purple hue. Majestically rising in the east, and peeping over the snow-clad peaks of Old Baldy, came the full moon, a mass seemingly of molten silver, and her radiance, with lavish hand, flooded peak and valley. The green of earth seemed deepened. The landscape took a strange quietness. The outer world was lost. It was a moment of such intense absorption that all other objects in the visible world seemed to vanish.

> "Heaven's ebon vault,
> Studded with stars unutterably bright,
> Through which the moon's unclouded grandeur rolls,
> Seems like a canopy which love has spread
> To curtain her sleeping world."

IV.

SANTA BARBARA.

A Contrast—The Old Mission Church—Chinese Labor—The Author of "Ramona"—Climate.

It would be hard to imagine a more radical change in the scene and feeling that one experiences in going from Pasadena to Santa Barbara. The former is bustle, life and activity. Eastern capital and brains have infused spirit into the every-day workings for business and enjoyment, while the latter is a sleepy old town, nestled under the mountain's protecting wing, with just enough Spanish flavor to make it romantic, and a general do-nothing air about the shops, streets, and public institutions. A man or woman who has been here ten years is an old resident, and any one who dates two decades is a veteran. The journey hither, which may be said to commence at Los Angeles, consumes about five hours. The route runs directly north to the coast for about one hundred miles. The country is low and flat, much of it uncultivated, and all for sale. Some newly planted orange groves and apricot trees are seen, as well as vast fields of mammoth cabbage and beet gardens. The road leaves the main line at Saugus and descends through the lovely valley of Santa Clara until the coast is reached at San Buenaventura, and for thirty miles you run along the sea.

How salty and bracing the air smells, and what a change from the flower-scented breezes we have left behind! The approach at night is a weird and beautiful sight. There is light enough to distinguish the overhanging presence of the Santa Ynez mountains. The harbor gleams with myriad lights, the town bristles with electric sparks, and opens eyes, arms and doors to give hospitable welcome to its best patron, the stranger. The houses are modern but unpretentious. They are mostly built of wood and generally surrounded by lovely gardens. Everything is as green and fresh as possible, and I seemed to realize the truth of a sentence to be found in the initial chapter of "Robert Elsmere," where we read, "Summer in the North is for Nature a time of expansion and of joy, as it is elsewhere; but there is none of that opulence, that sudden splendor and superabundance, which marks it in the South."

Thus, dear friends, in your snow-bound home, I feel how poorly words of mine can depict the charms of this summer-land. It is not that flower or shrub is newer or of sweeter perfume than are those which for a brief life we coax to grow, but it is the wildness and abandon of the scene, the out-door freedom, the present sunshine and oft recurring rain, the almost tropical warmth, the blue sky above— these are the fascinations of the spot. Here there are but few orange groves, but the graceful pepper trees line the streets, and are often covered with scarlet passion vines and bignonias of red and yellow hues. The magnolia grandiflora is in much favor as an ornamental tree, and grows to a great height. There is not what I would call one well ordered, carefully kept lawn in the whole place, but the wealth of disorder is picturesque. The possibilities are great, but they have ceased to excite our wonder.

The great attraction to visitors at Santa Barbara is the old mission church established in 1786. It is in a good state of preservation, and well worth a visit. Situated on a beautiful sunny slope, it is easy of access from the town. It is rambling and uncertain in plan, rooms having been added where and when most needed, without regard to unity. The walls are mostly of adobe mixed with brick. The facade, which rises above a wide doorway, is reached by a flight of low stone steps, and is guarded by twin towers, each with its quota of Spanish bells. You pull a cord, a quick tinkle tells that you are heard, and instantly the door opens and a solemn-faced, down-cast monk, with cowl and beads, obeys the summons and conducts you up the stone steps to the tower, whence a view of the surrounding country can be obtained.

How our eyes sweep over and drink in the loveliness! The white and red cottages and green trees gleam in the sunshine at our feet. The mountains are picturesque rather than grand, yet their coloring is exquisite, and the canyons leading among them are choked with bushes.

But above and overshadowing all, like a line of silver below the horizon, are the waters of the ocean, which upon its bosom holds mountains, islands, and many crafts of human freight and unlimited value. In such a scene one forgets that there are turmoils in this world, that killing winter ever reigns, that life is ever harsh and drear.

Meanwhile our guide, with fingers idly running over his rosary, and to whom the beauties of the day are as an oft-told tale, recounts the story of their old-time prosperity and power. The Indians were converted, then baptized and taught to labor for their own livelihood and the benefit of the Mission. In time some of the most expert among them became musicians and artists of such ability as to enable them to copy the Spanish pictures which adorn the church walls. It may not be artistic, but it seems to me that if the pictures which I saw are specimens of the old masters, before purchasing for adornment I will seek specimens of modern talent, for a more smoky, distressed-looking set of Madonnas I have never seen, and there failed to be a charm even in the face of the Holy Child.

Our attention was directed to an immense grapevine growing near the side of the church, older, said the Father, than the century, and producing annually eighty gallons of wine. "And what do you do with it?" I innocently inquired. "Drink it," was the ready response. I wish I could describe the merry twinkle in his eye and the unctuous gurgle of his tone as he added, "Did not St. Paul advise Timothy to 'drink no longer water, but use a little wine for thy stomach's sake'?" "Aye! but," I retorted, "did not one older even than the eminent apostle to the Gentiles command you to 'look not upon the wine when it is red; it biteth like an adder and stingeth like a serpent.'"

Remembering the performance of a woman in a garden many years ago, they will not, to this day, permit one of my sex to enter within. You can easily see it from the tower. It is only a queer old-fashioned place, interesting because forbidden. An exception, however, was made in the case of the Princess Louise, who not only entered but was permitted to make sketches.

There was a time in the history of the church when the men who dwelt here wielded an immense temporal and spiritual power, but, in the march of civilization, that has slipped from their hands, and to-day a mere handful of monks, with coarse garments, girded at the waist by a hempen cord, and wearing cowls, are all that are left to tell the tale of former greatness. I can fancy how the visit of the stranger and a few familiar words on worldly topics may come to them as a strain of long-forgotten music. They are men of like passions, education and hopes, and years of prayer and penitence do not blot out earthly desires and feelings. In their life of self-abnegation we trust they find happiness. Their lot is a free-will offering, and their deeds of mercy are many. A friendly bow of the head, and the cloistered door was closed; we went again to the world and the monk to his cell.

This is a country of many nationalities, and we are for the first time having a practical exposition of Chinese labor. All the servants in the house are of that despised race. The labor would not be called cheap, since the cook receives $30, the waiter $25, and the little boy of all work $10 per month. Capitally do they perform their allotted duties. I never saw hot cakes in such variety or of such excellence as the one who gives us our "daily bread" produces; and in the matter of desserts, the number he evolves from his celestial brain is infinite. Quick to learn, imitative in a rare degree, and with a capacity for calculation almost incredible, they will make a sharp bargain for the mistress. Those who have employed them say one Chinaman will accomplish more work than three women. They have retentive memories, and once told they neither neglect nor forget their duties.

I do not think the people of this section understand the niceties of domestic art as practiced in some households we have seen. A Chinaman would look with dismay at our sidewalk, and roll his eyes heavenward at the necessity of carrying things to the cellar; and I am not sure he would not leave, pig-tail and all, did the mistress undertake to interfere. He is absolutely monarch of all he surveys for the time being, with vegetables, meats and culinary apparatus within calling distance. His kitchen, like Aunt Chloe's, is a model of disorder. But "clarin'-up time" comes; and then the work, as he considers, done, he is off to Chinatown. His privileges are few; he is strong, willing and efficient, and whether as laundress, cook or chambermaid, he renders active and valuable aid, and makes the life of the mistress one of pleasure and not domestic warfare.

This region is alive with memories of the gifted authoress, "H. H.," as Mrs. Jackson was most generally known; and in the house where we now live she penned many chapters of her favorite work, "Ramona." I am sorry to say that the "bits of talk" which I have gathered are not of a nature to endear her to us, for they describe her in every-day life as dictatorial, possessing none of the womanly attributes, tabooing her own sex socially and intellectually, and caring only for the society of mankind. Sweet singer and delicate *raconteur* as she was, her home life was not an ideal one; and it was a noticeable fact that when she was presiding at the "dearest spot" her husband found it convenient to travel, and when he was there she was generally off on a philanthropic tour. But the laws of compensation hold good in domestic circles in this case, and her brilliant, suffering eyes were closed and her restless spirit stilled but a few months ere he married her niece, and now, as the story-book says, lives happily and contented. Mrs. Jackson had a hobby —the Indians and their wrongs—a most unpopular one in this region, and she rode it to death.

I was talking to an officer in the regular army recently in regard to the oppression of these children of the forest. An Eastern man by birth and education, he had been brought to look upon them as a deeply wronged race, and his earliest recollections were of a pious mother who labored assiduously and prayed fervently that they might be relieved from the tyranny of our government. Years of fierce and active conflict had given her son a fair estimate of their character, and he denounces them as fierce, vindictive and treacherous. No longer do they depend upon the white man for "fire-water," but among the arts of civilization they have learned to distil, from the corn in early autumn, a fiery drink called tizwin, which in a fermented state produces the wildest intoxication. Inflamed by this enemy they are quarrelsome and warlike and leaving their camps flee to the mountains and give themselves up to the wildest orgies. There are now entrenched in their fastnesses a bold, dissolute party, who are led by a well known desperado, committing crimes and causing much trouble to our government.

My informant very much doubted the propriety or usefulness of attempting to educate those who had attained manhood, and in support of his theory spoke of one named Constant, a graduate of Carlisle, and in high favor with Captain Pratt for talent and docility. When forced to act in the capacity of interpreter he exhibited such ignorance and obstinacy that the officer in command remonstrated with the surly fellow, and heard him mutter in reply: "Constant not speak English any more. Let his hair grow. Be Indian again." Thus are the benefits conferred by our government abused. If people would only labor for the "Greek who are at their doors," and let the heathen alone, how much more real good would be accomplished. Mrs. Jelleby and poor down-trodden Caddy is the truest satire of modern times.

In this odd, little, shut-off corner of the world distance seems increased and space multiplied, for both mail and female matter fail to reach us. It is said that the post-office here is conducted a little on the plan of Mr. Dickens' celebrated Circumlocution Office; where the requirement seemed to be the "art of perceiving how not to do it." The governmental fathers take no thought that the winter influx of visitors quadruples the mail matter in this little sea-board town, and with "Jeffersonian simplicity" and "Democratic economy" provide but an inefficient force to work upon the weighty accumulation. Once in a while, when threatened to be overwhelmed, it is said they quietly go down to the harbor and slip a whole budget of news into the Pacific. So we fancy the mermaids laughing over Mr. Williams' jokes in the *Herald*, and gleaning knowledge from our *Tribune* about poor old De Lesseps and his attempts to build a canal.

I have written this desultory chat without one word of reference to the climate. I did not mean to neglect what is in everybody's mouth. We are residents, having been here a couple of months, so I give it as my unbiased opinion that this is a most excellent place for healthy people, and the most capital spot for catching cold I have ever known. The variations of temperature are almost as great as in the much-abused East, and the utmost care must be observed to ensure health. I know this is rank heresy, for climate and town-lots are not to be trifled with in the presence of the natives. They are all frightfully in earnest, and with good cause, for they have risked their all on a bubble. Depend upon it, dear friends, Colonel Sellers is a fair prototype of the California land speculator. "There is millions in it," but how to get it out is the problem. It is said that one poor sick visitor was so incensed by the pictures that were drawn and no benefits received that he determined to leave the valley and seek the mountain top. Arriving at the base, he was told to "climb it." He left a wiser and a sadder man.

V.

EVERY-DAY TOPICS.

Picnicking in January—Ride to Carpenteria—Expense of Living, with Some Figures—Practical Definitions.

A PICNIC is generally considered a midsummer fête, but the one in which we assisted on the eighth day of January partook in nature of the modern institution, yet, paradoxical as it may seem, it was held in the winter-time. There was no mention of the old battle of New Orleans, or a certain birth-day we remembered, but the elements were so propitious we agreed to celebrate. The same old conditions were observed. The note of preparation sounded early in the morning; the inevitable delays and the usual laggards. Finally the wagons were heavily loaded, the stereotyped lunch stowed away, and off we went o'er hill and dale. Our destination was a great wilderness of a garden, which owed but little of its culture to any gardener save Nature; and while we sat and ate, over our heads was a canopy —leaf, bud and golden fruit in simultaneous perfection—and underneath a revel of every imaginable flower, forming a carpet of daphne, narcissus, heliotrope, anemones, clematis, bignonias and innumerable roses. Far away in the distance stretched the blue line of the Pacific, and we fancied its waves made music to our ears.

To us the drive to Carpenteria was one of newness and strange beauty. The road for many miles skirts the sea, and then is lost inland. Under the shadow of the foot-hills the lovely village of Montecito breaks upon our view. Here, watered by the dews and ripened by the sun, fruit, flower and vegetable grow in beauty and perfection. There seems to be a midsummer hum in the atmosphere. The place is drowsy, respectable and content. The mountains, no longer brown, but covered with a short brush, are always in sight, and the lights and shadows play upon them with charming effect.

But the sea, the grand old rolling ocean, ever changing yet always the same in power and might —that is the charm of this place, adding to its commercial importance. Strange crafts which have fattened on the spoils of other lands come and go from this port, and the great steamers sail in with stately grace, call for their living freight, and then are off for the isles of the far-away.

The beach is lined with eager children at play, who toss the sand and search for hidden treasures of shell and weed. The wharf is full of robust men, who fish and talk or idly sun themselves; and far out on the tossing waves are little cockle-shells, unerringly guided by those to whom fear is unknown.

It is not alone the mariner who loves the sea, for not more fondly do the Savoyards pine for the Swiss mountains, or the cockney for the sound of Bow-bells, than they who were born near it long to return and hear its voice. In dreams the children of the ocean renew their fealty. I think I have somewhere heard of a certain tribe of Arabs who have no name for the ocean, and when they came to the shore for the first time they asked with eager sadness, as if penetrated by the conviction of the superior beauty, "What is that desert of water, more beautiful than the land?" Is it not Proctor who sings,

"The sea! the sea! the open sea!
The blue, the fresh, the ever free!"

But to digress. Horseback-riding is the only amusement here, and it is indulged in by both sexes and all ages. From the tiny child, mounted on the gaily caparisoned donkey, to the sober, middle-aged matron, all ride. Some of the habits are of the most nondescript pattern; others, regulation style and exceedingly "good form." After a few lessons one and all adopt, or rather imitate, the Mexican style of gallop, and ride as though pursued or else in a fox-hunt. The paths which wind up the mountains, and over foot-hills and through canyons, are good, safe, and full of strange interest and weird beauty.

Being of a practical turn of mind, and some housewifely skill, I determined to acquaint myself with the expenses of living, and institute a comparison between this spot and home. Land, which certainly is plenty, and once was cheap, is never, even when surrounding the humblest dwelling, used for gardening purposes. The Chinaman seems to have a monopoly of the whole business, and each morning presents himself and well filled cart before your domicile. His vegetables are fresh, good in quality, and reasonable in price. Peas, which are sold in the pod by weight, at ten cents a pound, will, as the season advances, decrease to four cents; celery, three large stalks for ten cents; cabbage, two large heads for five cents; cauliflower, the finest I have ever seen grown, five cents apiece; potatoes, $1.25 per bushel; as for spinach, turnips, carrots, lettuce and radishes, there is no staple price—select as much as you require and pay "one bit" for the lot. Eggs average thirty cents per dozen; milk, ten cents per quart; butter, fifty cents per pound; turkeys and chickens, from eighteen to twenty-five cents per pound; and lamb and beef, not first quality by any means, from fifteen to eighteen cents per pound.

You will see that these prices are almost identical with those paid in Philadelphia markets, thus causing Santa Barbara, to any other than a vegetarian, to be an expensive place in which to live. The prices paid in Atchison, Kansas, were to me matters of astonishment and delight. Every householder there should in time become a millionaire, with butter at eighteen cents per pound; turkeys and chickens, already dressed, at from eight to ten cents per pound; and meat, milk and eggs decreasing in price in the same ratio. If the Kansans were wide-awake they would advertise their state as a health resort; or, better still, get up a "boom," and then see if prices would not inflate.

This is a very matter-of-fact chapter, as all who read it will agree, so I will continue to discuss homely, every-day topics, intending in time to change location, and then give revel to my imagination. The reformer or suggester has always an ungracious task; but were I a lexicographer, in my next dictionary some definitions would be amended to suit California soil and times and to open the eyes of travelers. In other words, I would call things by their right names, and they would read in this wise:

Ranch—A farm, large or small.

Hacienda—A low, tumble-down, disreputable-looking building.

Senorita—An ill-favored woman.

Mexican—An idle, dissolute fellow.

Chinaman—An honest, hard-working laborer.

Canyon—A ravine.

Oranges—A sour fruit, which we would scorn at home; picked while unripe, on account of the cupidity of the owner.

Then, in the new geography which I would issue, I would describe the state as possessing the greatest natural advantages of scenery, soil and climate, with at least ten different varieties of weather; where the dress of the natives consists of baggy trousers, a silk handkerchief for neck-tie, and a broad sombrero for head-gear; whose occupation is nothing, and whose aims and aspirations are of kindred ilk. When asked, What do they subsist on? the reply would be: "Climate and strangers." And when the supply of the latter fails they will starve or, what in their minds would be infinitely more humiliating, have to work.

Then this little pocket-manual of mine would continue: "For what is Pasadena celebrated?" "Its view." "What are the distinguishing traits of Santa Barbara?" "The sea." "What does Riverside produce?" "Very good oranges, when allowed to ripen." "What are the attractions of San Diego?" "The beach and a mammoth hotel." "Does this country produce much fruit?" "Yes; but it is all consumed in the East."

You see, a few plain statements in books of instruction would teach travelers what to expect, and that they would know that they would be alternately roasted and frozen; that their baggage would be weighed and its transportation charged; that railroad fares are at the rate of ten cents per mile; and that you can buy a ticket at Atchison, Kansas, to San Francisco, six hundred miles away, for the same price you pay to Los Angeles.

Consumptives take more colds here, if they stay in-doors in the damp houses, than they would at the East in a variable temperature; but let them be sufficiently strong to enjoy out-door life and exercise, and then the benefit begins. The houses here have no cellars. Ice is not in general use. The meat-safe is suspended to the limb of a tree, and the curative properties of the air will preserve the contents many days.

On Sunday afternoon we walked through the lovely undulating country to the Mission, where at three o'clock the monks chant the vesper service. The day was balmy and our gait a brisk one, but in no very devotional frame of mind we took our seats in a chapel which would vie with a vault in dampness, and which, like Mr. Mantilini's description, was "moist and unpleasant."

The season thus far is the ideal one. The rains have not been too frequent, but just the right kind to start vegetation. We read that you of the Atlantic coast are having cyclones and tornadoes, with dreadful loss of life; and we, who are in this region of earthquakes, send you words of sympathy.

It is almost impossible to get a clear, concise, or, we had almost said, truthful statement in regard to anything. They always tell you what has been, and prophesy what will come. The future months are promised full of richness. We hope to be here to see and describe this resurrection of the deciduous trees, and note the peach, almond, apricot, pear and olive in their bloom and beauty, and look upon the hill-side when covered with the grape, and enjoy the odor of its blossom as like a sweet-smelling incense it ascends heavenward.

Traveling is indeed a liberal education, but the study of humanity is more interesting than much scenery. The various motives which have influenced people to leave their firesides, the impressions which things both common-place and wonderful make upon them, are a study. The enthusiasm in some, the lack of interest which others manifest, all go to make up the panorama. Do you remember the poor victim who had been dragged hither and yon in search of the beautiful, and who, in despair, asked a friend in melancholy tone, "Do you admire the beauties of nature? As for me, I abhor them!" Fancy the strident emphasis on the last sentence.

A good traveler is not always active or bustling, but one whose judgment selects what is really wonderful, enjoys it, and moderates his raptures. He gives no information unsolicited, but makes himself generally agreeable, neither grumbling at discomforts nor drawing invidious comparisons with other scenes.

As regards the conduct of my own sex, I feel like saying with Pepys in his immortal diary, and I hope to have the benefit of a quotation, "But, Lord! what poor stuff it was they did talk." Actual contact with a spot is oft-times disenchanting. I cite the case of a romantic, middle-aged female, who put herself to considerable trouble and expense that she might visit Camulos and bring away some memento of " H. H." Mrs. Jackson visited the spot but once, and then remained one hour. Her great novel, the effort of her life, was written in the second-story front room of the boarding-house in which I lodge, and her heroine, Ramona Ortnega, was named in honor of a servant then employed there. Alas, for fame and relic-hunters!

VI.

RIVERSIDE.

Orange Cultivation—The Land Agent—San Diego—Coronado Beach—Personal.

RIVERSIDE is undoubtedly the centre of orange cultivation, and the perfection of the system as well as the superiority of the fruit is acknowledged by all who visit there. The town proper amounts to nothing. It has the usual pretentious business street, electric lights, street railways, and the foundations for a monster hotel. The groves and drives are for beauty and variety beyond description. Conceiving the idea of a town, and observing the very favorable conditions of temperature, about twelve years ago a land improvement company bought the tract, divided it into sections and lots, and began to beautify it by planting the trees which are now in luxuriant growth. Magnolia avenue, which is seven miles long, is at least one hundred and twenty feet wide, and bounded on either side by hedges of palm, cypress, gravilla, magnolia and eucalyptus, these hedges half concealing yet revealing continuous orchards of orange, olive, lemon, lime, apricot, and vineyards unending, all reposing in the sunshine of a matchless sky. Here the groves are laid out with almost mathematical accuracy. The trees are stout and thrifty, the hedges well trimmed—some in fanciful shapes, the weeds kept down, and the dwellings rose-embowered and of a neat cottage pattern. It is the home of thrift and prosperity. The lack of water is the great and vexing question of this section, but sagacious minds here builded as they knew and expended millions of dollars in an improved system of irrigation, and have constructed miles of what they term flumes—in reality shallow ditches—from which at regular distances the water can be drawn, and the whole surface of the land flooded about once in five weeks. The season termed "rainy" here is certainly a misnomer, without it is so called in contradistinction to the summer, when for five months not a drop falls, and consequently summer tourists see naught but what is brown and parched. We have—I speak from actual experience—been in the state more than two months, and have had but three rainy days. The most assiduous care is taken to water gardens and lawns, but from the heavens there is literally no drop.

No oranges which we have found in California equal the celebrated fruit of Indian river, Florida. I care not how many medals may have been awarded at rival expositions, the fact remains that they are thick-skinned and sour to the taste. About six years ago there was introduced at Riverside the Washington Navel, the trees of which are now in good bearing condition and the fruit of fine size and quality. We visited the groves, saw them picked, and paid therefor sixty cents a dozen. So you see even here, with a crop of millions, the price is the same as at home. It is the object of the owners here to keep their merchandise until the Florida product is sold, and with this end in view they allow it to remain on the tree as long as possible, and then put it in refrigerator-rooms built and especially adapted for its preservation.

Outside the drives there is nothing to interest or detain the visitor more than a few hours here. The foundations of a magnificent hotel on a commanding site on the Rubideau mountains, overlooking the Santa Anna river and the town, have been laid, but like the one at Los Angeles, intended to accommodate the entire traveling public, the work has progressed only as far as the foundation, and is now, for lack of capital, totally abandoned. To tell the plain truth, the whole season here has been a lamentable failure. At first the lack of visitors was ascribed to the fact that the male population could not or would not leave home until after casting the Presidential vote; next, the potential claims of the holidays were urged; but now the season wanes, the country is once more saved, and still they come not, and the eyes of the hotel-keepers wax weary with much and fruitless watching, and their tongues are strangely silent, for bankruptcy stares them in the face. In the San Gabriel valley stands one hostlerie in a situation of unequalled beauty, with mountain and fertile plain for its boundaries, solitary and alone. On the side of the Sierre Madre mountains is perched the Villa, among orange groves, and with a world of romantic loveliness before it, and it holds a dozen guests. Almost at the mouth of the canyon we found the Sanitarium, a quaint little cottage built of the Arroyo, and with all the ingenious contrivances of sun-baths, swings and tents for those who need a physician, and there were four patients. But why multiply cases, and thus spy out the poverty of the land?

A woman living near Ventura was known to have realized a hundred thousand dollars by her land speculations, and not content with her success she conceived the idea of getting up another "boom." She chartered a train from San Francisco, five hundred miles away, gave free ride, free lunch, and with a band of music in attendance made the air jubilant for her great land sale. The cars were crowded, and the agents did not give away tickets indiscriminately; her food was eaten, the music was sweetly discoursed, but there were no bids; she sold not one lot; and the price she paid for the experiment was twenty thousand dollars. I should think that much bought wit might go a great ways; in fact, suffice for a whole county.

The greatest curiosity I have seen in this region of many wonderful things is the land agent, and I have yet to find his equal in urbanity, good nature, volubility, and ability to answer questions whether relating to things temporal or spiritual. Twice a week there are little railway excursions to old Mexico, the road leading through such attractive names as Chula Vista, Tia Juana, and Otay. We first stopped at National City, and the inspection we made of the olive oil manufactory was both instructive and pleasing. The greatest cleanliness is observed lest the flavor of the oil be vitiated. The groves are on every side, and in proper season the little green berry or fruit is picked and carefully dried to extract the water. Next it is subjected to grinding and great pressure, and the pure oil is obtained. After a careful process of filtration it is bottled and, the agents claim, the only pure oil in the world obtained. All other, they say, is adulterated with cotton seed. This has a golden hue, as clear as pure water, and sells here for two dollars a bottle which certainly does not contain a quart.

But to resume. The object of the excursion, which is a ridiculously cheap one, is of course to sell land, and with this end in view a couple of these sleek oily-tongued agents are always on board each train. Some one made inquiry in regard to oranges; a basketful was produced, divided and passed around. Another spoke of olives; a tin pail of them appeared, and their nutritious qualities in comparison to beef steak were ably discussed. We had all questions, civil, religious and moral, ably debated, and conclusive reasons given when we saw a vacant house why the owners had moved away. There happened to be in our party two well-known men of means. By some wonderful instinct these fellows discovered the fact. Never were men such objects of devotion; information was given unasked; questions were replied to almost before propounded; no amount of quizzing produced the slightest shade of perturbation; from the introduction to the final farewell it was all smoothness and urbanity, and not one single cent profit.

We all agreed with them that as a home for the poor or middle class, this stands unrivalled. With so few radical changes of temperature, fuel, excepting for cooking purposes, is unnecessary. The same clothing may be worn all the year, and the land with but little tilling will produce abundantly. Our informant described four crops of potatoes annually, each tuber the size of a bowl, but we drew the line at two yields, and think that the amateur farmer would be satisfied with that. Any one of means who is used to the refinements of life, who loves books, sermons, pictures, operas, theatres, and a thousand things which go to make up the sum total of a pleasant existence, had better remain East. There is nothing here but the climate and flowers to repay you for what you leave behind. This is not a land for enjoyment. It is too new. The lines are yet hard.

The school houses all over the state are such as excite surprise, and meet with much commendation. They are well built, airy, and surrounded by large play-grounds. In fact, the one at Riverside is quite a model of architectural beauty. This alone will create a need, and should draw many young men and women to this section, who, realizing that here, as in every other place, work is a necessity, will secure a livelihood and assure their happiness and success.

The distance from Riverside to San Diego is about one hundred miles, through a country of great beauty and romantic interest. The mountains are always in sight, many of the peaks glistening with snow. There are a few streams. All else is green meadow land, and wild unexplored canyons. The modest little wild flowers are beginning to hold up their dainty heads, and in some fields the poppies, or, as we call them, escholtzias, are spread out like a cloth of gold. Did you ever think of the apparent inconsistency of riding through a country with fruit and flowers in perfection, yet clad in warm winter garb; of crossing rippling streams, yet looking at ice and snow upon the land nearest the sun? We do it each day, and enjoy while we can not explain the anomaly.

Ramona has thrown the glamour of romance over all this region, and as we enter Temecula canyon we recall her wild flight with Alessandro, and think of the days of concealment here afforded them, while in the silvery note of every wood-dove we seem to hear the plaintiff call "Majella." For eighteen miles the railway winds through the canyon, sometimes climbing its sides, then skirting the cliff, and often darting in wild and tortuous manner along some sparkling, babbling brook. What Scott did for his native land "H. H." has given to this section, and the "bits of travel" she here gathered have gone far and wide and made the region known and loved. Alessandro, as she portrayed him, was clearly a picture of the imagination. No Indian here is his prototype. Her story is faulty, but her descriptions of the places are life-like and most attractive.

The shore of the Pacific ocean for many miles north of San Diego is a succession of rounding promontories, walling the mouths of canyons, down which small streams run to the sea. These ravines are filled with oak trees. Beginning at little more than rifts in the ground, they widen and deepen till at their mouths they show a beautiful crescent of shining beach sometimes an eighth of a mile long.

San Diego is the least attractive of all the towns we have yet seen. Its one great feature and boast is its climate, which annually attracts thousands. It is dirty and dusty, and as some one wittily remarked, "Here there is a genuine rise in real estate." The whole interest of the place centers around the hotel Del Coronado, which is built almost in the sea, and which with its glass porches, balconies, attractive grounds and good service, certainly is a place at which the tired wanderer can find rest.

People bathe here every day, but I doubt whether it is comfortable or profitable to the body. The grounds, only a year old, are beautifully laid out, and the hedges of Marguerites miracles of snowy bloom. Coronado is yet in its infancy; a few years of care will make it a garden spot. Think of the advantages such a seaport possesses. It is in reality an all-the-year-round resort.

Many incidents in regard to the people one meets

in six months of travel might make entertaining reading, but in showing up the faults and foibles of others we are apt to forget our own. Still, it is always an interesting study to watch prominent people, and, if possible, learn something which the daily journals have not found out. When it was noised about that one of Boston's many-millioned citizens was en route for the Pacific slope, every one was on the *qui vive* to see him, and there was considerable curiosity as to how he would deport himself. True, the money was only his by inheritance; we do not know that he had ability to make a single dollar. But he is so "awfully" rich as to be almost a curiosity. In our Sunday night discourse, with this gentleman for the text, some one said, You might judge what the Lord thought of money when you saw what kind of men he bestowed it upon. And thus we debated pro and con on the desire for wealth and its relations to the Kingdom of Heaven. Well, he had to come in the ordinary way, although he had a special car, in which they say he was so lonely that after two days he wished himself back to Boston and beans. However, after various waitings, and frequently being side-tracked, and the hundred detentions which are inevitable on a long journey, he arrived, and we read in open-eyed wonder: Mr. So-and-so and valet; Mrs. So-and-so and maid; Master So-and-so and governess. Thus panoplied, do you wonder they were not having a good time? As for the heir apparent, I fancied he looked wistfully at the other boys and girls when he was led out to get his proper portion of air by his severe-eyed duenna. I am not sure but that a little such discipline as he would gain in a few hours' rough-and-tumble would be good for him, and teach him that other boys had active legs and vicious fists ready to be called into action when provoked.

Very different was the conduct of another man, whose name is familiar to the world as a representative of wealth and commercial importance in New York. His worldly possessions are fabulous, but his manners are the plainest. He and his wife, unattended, came to see the country, and their good points of observation, ability to ask questions, and uncommon discernment, made their trip a profitable one. Now I am not going to mention the name, which is best known in New York both in shipping and social circles, but I am going to tell a little anecdote which, if known, might cause merriment among his friends. En route for Coronado the street cars were full, and our many-times millionaire waived his right to a seat, and shared the front platform with many others. One of the duties of the driver is to collect the fares, and during his temporary absence our friend seized the lines, managed the brake, took one passenger on, and wickedly nodding his head at me wanted to know if I did not wish to get off. He took such evident pleasure in the whole performance that I would have liked to photograph him in the discharge of the duty.

Moody and Sam Jones have both been here wrestling with Satan and the sinners of the coast. I believe they met with great success, as far as crowded houses, heavy contributions and free newspaper advertisements go. As for the practical results I can see no marked improvement, either in the habits or dealings of their converts. They tell a good story, which I think is new; it certainly is true, and will do to close this desultory chat.

At one of the meetings at which unusual interest had been manifested, the customary request was made that those suffering from a particularly heavy burden should stand up and ask for the prayers of the assembled multitude. After a few moments' silence a tall, lank individual arose, and in a voice choked by emotion asked in a faltering tone that the prayers of the congregation might be offered for his mother-in-law. At first there was a smile, then a titter, and finally, grave religious body as it was, the whole audience broke into a roar that would not have disgraced a first-class minstrel show. It was every man's burden.

A few days more and we will have sailed through the Silver Gate and out upon the bosom of the Pacific for another port; after which we go into the Ojai Valley, and in that secluded spot, the "world forgetting and the world forgot," will write whereof we see.

VII.

OJAI VALLEY.

Rural Scenes—Honey Industry—Comforts and Discomforts—Personal Incidents.

The February weather for the last few days had been a mortification to the inhabitants and a disappointment to the visitors. We were assured on every side that the proper amount of rain-fall had been received, but, unfortunately, all at one time; consequently the drought of the last six weeks, while it did not seem to interfere with the growth of fruit or flowers had been productive of both dust and considerable discomfort. Added to this, a high, cold wind prevailed for several days, which was supplemented by sufficient frost to make bananas, callas, cannas, nasturtiums and other tender plants droop their heads, and prove to us that tropical and semi-tropical were terms which existed only in name; we had indubitable proof that we were not below the frost-line. Many of the mountain-tops were quite hoary, but there was no talk of sleds or snow-shoes.

The rain, like every other blessing, came in time to those who waited for it. A series of soft, gentle showers descended, cheering the heart of nature, giving new vigor to shrub and meadow-land, and waking to activity the stranger and sojourner within the gates. We decided it best to no longer postpone the projected trip to the Ojai, which could be made in three days, in an open wagon, drawn by four stout, sure-footed horses, guided by a skillful driver.

Early on a Tuesday we made ready for the start. The almanac marked midwinter, the air promised midsummer, and we enjoyed the rare combination of sea and mountain breezes, for our road led in the direction of Montecito, past Carpenteria, near the beach, where a line of sand dunes, overgrown with trailing vines and flowers, throw into bold relief the back-ground of the ocean. The farmers were, with the aid of their mowing-machines, cutting the grass, or rather what is known as alfalfa. The plowmen were busily at work, the truckmen putting in seeds and vines; trimming, pruning and budding were all in active operation. We also passed great patches of strawberry plants, hanging full of medium-sized fruit.

A few, and only a few, peach and apricot blossoms were peeping out. We had had continual spring, but now it seemed to portend that summer was nigh. The Casitas mountains, high, impenetrable and overpowering, were before us. Our way lay through their heart, so we slowly climbed, each moment revealing new beauties and fresh delights, until the summit was gained. The sturdy live and white oaks, the hardy sycamore, festooned with swaying clusters of Spanish moss—the home of the traditional mistletoe—and dark emerald pines, covered both hill and valley; while an exquisite carpet of wild-flowers, which defies description, peeped from nook and crevice, and seemed to nod a glad welcome. In every direction there was nothing but verdure—the green of the ferns intensified by the oaks, and that of the trees by the shrubs on the mountain slopes. The delicate, crape-like blossom of the wild cucumber wreathed the trunks of gnarled old trees; the scarlet bunch-berries, so much resembling holly, appeared to get a more fiery tint from the midday sun; and the graceful morning-glory, with its pink-veined bell, seemed to run and mock us in wild, unrestrained beauty. The rich purple of the blossom of the wild onion mingled and strongly contrasted with the golden poppy, and the mauve clusters of the lilac stood by the side of the scarlet gooseberry, while a pink cluster resembling laburnum diffused a delicate aroma. There were ox-eyed daisies flaunting their gay hues, anemones, pæonies, columbines, and a thousand unnamed varieties. A botanist would have raved over new specimens, and diving into their hearts announced name, class and species; we were neophytes at Nature's shrine, and gathered them for their loveliness and delicious odor. Occasionally a tiny squirrel would start at our approach, a blue-bird pipe its little lay, or a gopher pop out of its earthy home; then a great flock of black birds would circle over our heads, as though we had disturbed their council. Like Selkirk, we were "out of humanity's reach."

And thus the hours rolled on. The world was at our feet. This grandeur was a new and fresh lesson. We seemed near Heaven. Here had been no jar save from the elements. How our lungs expanded with great draughts of pure mountain air. What health and life seemed at our call. Sometimes the way was dangerous in its winding, and the edge of the precipice perilously near, but on we sped though chasms were ready to engulf us, until

Casitas Pass was reached and the first stage of our journey safely accomplished.

A little after noon we came to a clearing, or, by courtesy, half-way house, where for an hour we stopped to refresh both man and beast. It was a fresh, green valley, almost park-like in appearance, thickly studded with majestic oaks. The accommodations were primitive, as becomes the forest. An overhanging tree, a rude table and some refuse boxes were the equipment. We ate with thankful hearts and sharpened appetites, and the feast was better than the proverbial stalled ox or fatted calf. The owner of what was termed the ranch came to us with proffers of tea and milk. In the distance was his cabin, a one-story wooden house, built to ensure free circulation of air. I am not sure there were any windows, but the chinks would let plenty of light in; and, as far as I could judge, they spent more time out than in-doors. Excepting a few chickens there was no sign of animal life, nor of vegetable; yet they said they lived on quail, rabbit and fowl. Certainly their appearance denoted neither restriction in diet nor starvation. From our standpoint, these people possessed not one comfort, yet at the door stood in smiling welcome the wife, a comely Mexican woman, and by her side and in her arms two sturdy, healthy specimens of infantine beauty, whose dancing black eyes, rosy cheeks and stout limbs would have gladdened any mother's heart. What splendid specimens they were, and what a good start in life to be endowed with its best capital—health. I patted the one little head and asked her name. "Helen," she timidly replied, and my heart warmed toward the tiny stranger, for at roll-call two of our party would answer to that summons. The man, a mixture of Spanish and American, was evidently of the better class, and had a medium education. He was a farmer on a small scale, his specialty being bees and the manufacture of honey. This delicious syrup is found in perfection here, and is world-renowned, for the cunning little manufacturers feeding upon the wild flowers make a product unequalled in flavor and purity. On a sunny slope was the apiary and the various appliances. They were at a reasonable distance, and for once we manifested no desire to approach or inspect, but were satisfied with such information as the proprietor could give us.

We interrogated him in regard to the yield, and heard with open-eyed astonishment that he annually produced and sent to market about eight tons. Now a bee is the synonym for industry, and the "busy" one of the spelling-book one of the earliest lessons imparted to the infant mind; but look at the insect and his machinery, and then think of eight tons! It was a whopper. I cannot understand the desire of these people to overrate everything. The tale would be big enough and quite as surprising if they would stick to fact.

And just here I would like to tell a story which they locate in Los Angeles. It appears that a Californian, desirous of impressing a stranger with the natural advantages and perfections of that city, declared that it possessed every virtue known to the civilized world. Finally, wearied with the length, or rather size, of the narrative, the editor asked, "Can you think of anything that you do not possess right here?" "Well," said he of the sleek tongue, "a little more water would be advantageous, and our society might be improved." "My friend," was the response, "those two elements are all that is needed to render a place not mentioned to 'ears polite' habitable." That is a wicked tale, but it is not a pointless one, and therein is the merit. It has a moral.

Let us not digress so far from the scene of rural beauty, but turn from man and civilization to the mountain-side, on which the sage-brush grows and the garden herb, in common parlance "old man," waves in the breeze. We ford innumerable brooks, or, as our driver says, we cross one stream a score of times. For miles we drive through the clearing, and then our way will lie through groves of walnut, apricot and peach trees; all sturdy, healthy, and ready to produce. How the heart of the owner must swell when he gazes on the sight. The outlay is slight and his reward sure and profitable. The elements help rather than hinder his work, and so popular are his products that the world is his market. Here there are no orange groves. A citrus belt is found in the Upper Ojai, where neither fertilizer nor irrigation is needed, the crop certain but small, peculiar in flavor and very sweet.

It was nearly sundown when, tired and delighted, we reached Nordhoff, and in a few minutes our journey was ended and we alighted at Oak Glen cottages. The last half of the ride was as easy as the first, for the road led down the mountain by easy grades. It is a quiet and retired place, where there is but little to do but admire and study nature. Seemingly near but some distance from the base of the mountain you sit and gaze and long to climb the sides. Situated that they catch and greet the first gleam of the morning sun, his last rays rest upon them like a benison. So environed is Ojai that "no chilling wind or poisonous breath" can reach it; the air is fresh, mild and dry. Its visitors are invalids, tourists and sportsmen.

The place is entirely bucolic, and the pleasures of the most innocent, restful kind. You sit in the sunlight, listen to the hum of the bees, watch the cows stand in green pasture-fields, and hear the song of the birds, and your day's work is done. There is here the greatest air of perfect rest and quiet I have ever seen. There is literally no sound; the world is too far away. The hotel accommodations are plain, clean and neat. There is an abundance of good milk and cream and sweet, light bread. A fire is necessary night and morning and gives you a cheerful welcome. A couple of years ago, when the "boom" was in progress, every one was so wild that they neglected to cut and dry the customary supply of fire-wood. Is it not Sterne who says "God tempers the wind to the shorn lamb"? So, providentially, just at this time an asphaltum was discovered which burns freely, and spread among green wood quickly ignites, making a fire which for easy kindling, warmth and beauty has no equal. I have heard of people who die of overwork, of those who are the prey of *ennui*, but I think any one who would go to the Ojai alone, or for an indefinite time, would pass away from too much rest.

In this memorable journey of mine, which has embraced a period of five months, I have met, I trust without being intrusive, a great variety of characters. Some have too much money, others too much time, each equally objects of pity. At Coronado it was my habit to stray into the west parlor, and invariably alone watch the god of day as he set in what might aptly be called "a sea of glory." I noticed one evening a very complaisant old man, who was evidently so lonely that he opened a conversation, and finding a willing listener told me some of the incidents of what had been rather a varied life. From the story I gathered that he was past middle age, rich and childless, roaming over the world in search of contentment and finding it not. He had had four beautiful homes in, it might almost be said, the four quarters of the continent, and he was tired and lonely in them all. His wife was somewhat younger, and neither had a near deserving relative, and the man was morose and sorrowful at the thought of leaving his possessions. He looked so forlorn that I thought a little poetry might cheer him, so from out the store-house of memory I recited him a verse which is applicable in many cases, and runs in this wise:

> "He saved, and he saved, and he saved,
> Economical, good Mr. Husband;
> And when he had got all he craved,
> It went to his wife's second husband."

It was a word fitly spoken, and I wish you could have heard him laugh. The sentiment was so pointed that he understood, and it touched him. He had me repeat it, and we laughed together. This produced a fairer understanding, and we continued our talk. Finally, I startled him by saying, as though perfectly certain of my ground, "You are a Democrat." The sleek silk hat which he had been so assiduously polishing slipped from his grasp, and he thought me a mind-reader or clairvoyant, for no word of political import had passed between us. It was simply that I never saw a man with his conservative views on every subject who had not those affiliations, and he acknowledged that in his whole life he had voted the straight Democratic ticket. Had I been as candid and confidential as he, I would have said that all my associations had been with the other party, and as a child I had been taught that there was a triumvirate of monsters—rum, a certain horned gentleman, and the Democrats—and so faithfully had I learned the lesson, that while I expected to go to Heaven disfranchised, my voice was always potential for Republicans and their measures. Here was a man with the ability and power to do good in the world, yet so incapable and halting that opportunities and life would soon slip away. He told me that he suffered with such an intense sense of desolation that sometimes he thought he would give anything he possessed for some of his own kin to come to him, that he might help them and in return have their sympathy and love. That is the secret of many lives—loneliness, lack of home ties, discontent, and finally oblivion. I have seen both men and women with whom I would not barter the joy and crown of my motherhood for their vast possessions, and far down in our heart of hearts is a joy and gladness when we think of the little ones to follow in our foot-steps, it may be for ill, we trust and hope for good. Was it not a proud woman who said of her child, "He is homely, but he is my own." There comes to me now and then a little scrawl of a few words and many blots. The writing is not faultless, and much is left to the imagination. There is no startling intelligence contained therein, although time without stint has been given to the composition; but the words, "Dear grandma, we miss you," are more to me than the most eloquent utterances of other pens —for the heart which prompted it is loyal and still unsullied by the world. I do not believe that absence conquers love. It heightens it. With me the poverty of the present life stands out in bold relief against the wealth of affection which the past held, and which I know the future possesses.

VIII.

RETURN TO SANTA BARBARA.

Two Kinds of Visitors—Some Attractions—Poor Tomasso—Unity Chapel.

THERE are two sorts of visitors who go to Santa Barbara. The one kind, because it is set down in the itinerary as the proper thing to do; and the other, and by far the larger class, who confess the charm of the humble seaport, and love to linger weeks among her gardens and rose-embowered cottages, or walk upon the beach in search of such treasures as the sea may wash to their feet. It were worse than idle to explain to the first named the attractions of the place. They came and saw the mountains, praised or condemned the hotel, looked upon the waves, took a few lovely drives, and then hurried northward to the noise and bustle of the great city.

We came for rest and healing, and drew strength from the mild, balmy air; knew every nook and corner of the land; could find the finest and gayest-hued wild flowers; saw the mountains when touched with the Alpen glow; hunted up old Mexican women and unearthed their marvellous drawn-work; were indefatigable in our search for water-baskets and Navajo blankets; saw everything in a roseate light; and for six midwinter weeks revelled in the sunshine of May.

The society of the town is excellent, composed as it is of men and women of worth and culture. The fortnightly Assembly serves to introduce you to that element. The sewing societies of the different churches invite all interested to join that industry. When I saw the basket, so similar to the familiar one so many miles away, and noted that the contents were aprons, cushions, caps, needle-books, umbrella-cases and pen-wipers, all making ready for an Easter sale, my heart grew tender, and I thought of the universal bond which led us to labor together.

Then many hours can be spent in inspecting the process of stamping leather, many mementoes of which are carried away; or a morning will swiftly pass while listening to Kendrick, he of the smooth tongue and guileless story, himself a greater curiosity than his varied tales. And thus the days roll by.

The place has both traditions and romances, and the great grape-vine which is such a curiosity is said to have sprung from a twig which served as a whip for a fair equestrienne, who in a sportive moment stuck it in the ground. It grew and thrived, and now is a marvel of beauty, strength and productiveness.

Another and more plaintive tale is that of old Tomasso, who in the early days of the century came from Spain to prepare in this New World of unknown riches a home for the one he hoped to wed. Faithfully and patiently he labored for her, and when all was ready the message went for her to come. He was humble and unlettered, but his heart was aglow with devotion, and the tiny home he had reared looked charming to the lover's eye. The stately vessel which was to bring the fair one came gallantly into the harbor, but there was no answer to his signal, and sadly and with much emotion the rough sailors told their tale. She who started buoyant in spirits, the embodiment of health, had died in mid-ocean, and in that great cemetery of buried hopes and many loved ones she sank to rest. Poor Tomasso! one hour a light-hearted boy, the next a broken-hearted man. Sadly he listened to the story.

It was so plain that there was no ground for hope. Vacantly he gazed upon the scene, and then turned towards the home which his industry and love had created. From that day his mind was a blank, and year after year he wandered along the beach, always expectant yet never satisfied, until one morning they found him dead, his face oceanward, his hands reaching out as though to clasp some familiar object, and his spirit with her he had so faithfully mourned.

Then on Sunday. Oh! the delight of the day to join the worshiping throng at Unity Chapel and listen to the marvellous eloquence of one who preaches, in his reasonable and poetic fashion, the glowing doctrine of liberal Christianity; who pleads for charity, not as mere alms-giving, but the ministering to and elevating our fellow-men; who draws his comparisons from the bee, the flower, the babbling brook, and awakens by his earnestness that true spirit of religion which teaches us all to be better men and women. Surely such a spirit as he manifests will bring its reward.

The little chapel is plain, almost a rude structure. The decorations are a bunch of roses, or a branch of vine gorgeous with scarlet blossoms. There is no remarkable singing or pretentious service, but the congregation fill every nook and corner of the edifice, and listen with rapt attention to the persuasive words of truth which fall from the lips of this gifted young man. Moody with his pleading eloquence, and Sam Jones by his abuse, may produce a religious convulsion on the Pacific slope, yet I doubt whether any good or permanent benefit will accrue from their labors. Yet why do I doubt, since one morning in market a certain man, in response to an inquiry regarding some pears he had for sale, remarked, with a merry twinkle in his eye and an under-current of fun in his tone, "No, they are not Winter Nelis. I have sold lots of them under that name; but I heard Sam Jones last night, and I can not tell a lie."

Thus, in this simple, home-like fashion, the winter months have glided by. We have known neither rain, snow, nor chilly breath. It has been a summer holiday, in which health and strength have come to us.

IX.

CHINATOWN.

San Francisco—But More About Chinatown—A Wide Field for Missionary Labor.

SHAKING the dust of Santa Barbara off our feet and gowns, with many regrets at leaving new-found friends, we pass on toward the northern portion of California—trusting in that oft-quoted region to find fresh pleasures and delights. The ride to Newhall is a lovely combination of mountain and sea. Many of the fields were ablaze with yellow flowers, and on every side were farmers with plow and seed. At Saugus we leave orange groves, and nearly every mark of civilization fades away when we reach and traverse the Mojave desert, running for hours amid arid plains, with no sign of vegetation save a few cacti and yucca palms. Once in a while we reach the hut of a Chinaman, but greater desolation than the route furnishes does not exist.

Near Pixley some of the timid inquire in regard to the modes of protection in case of assault. *We* quiet their fears, *they* hide both money and jewelry, *all* slept the sleep of the just, and awoke refreshed and safe.

The country near and around San Francisco is well cultivated and attractive. The large farms with substantial buildings prove thrift and prosperity. Thus early in March vegetation is advanced in about the same degree as in the section we had just left. The peach and almond trees are in full bloom, and the early salads, peas and strawberries ready for use. In the market there is the usual display of things, fresh and green. The poultry is fine in quality and nicely prepared. Some splendid specimens of pineapples were offered at a dollar apiece, while pears which had been kept all winter in refrigerator rooms found ready sale at five cents, but were hard and entirely wanting in flavor. Oysters, poor, miserable specimens, are not much sought after, and form a decided contrast to the delicious bivalve with which we are so well acquainted.

San Francisco, before a sealed book to us, we lived to know and admire to the same extent as all who had preceded us. We rode up and down her hills upon the wonderful cable cars which so delight every traveler's heart; saw Nob Hill, where men live who went to bed poor and awoke rich and famous; visited the Presidio; crossed the wonderful bay, second only to Naples; and saw Oakland, full of lovely homes and flowers.

The streets of this city are full of a gaily dressed throng. Every one is in a hurry. The business part is an aggregation of large, well built structures, while the private houses manifest taste and a liberal expenditure of money. But no dwelling, no matter how elaborate, when constructed of wood, can, in our opinion, vie with the costly stone structures which adorn Eastern cities. The trees and shrubs, hardy and semi-tropical, the flowers and graceful vines, which adorn and flourish both winter and summer, make an ornamental prettiness new and agreeable to us.

Chinatown, the abomination of mankind, is dear to the heart of every woman, and her farewell visits to that attractive locality are as frequent as those of a retiring prima donna. Dilapidated in appearance, with streets narrow and exceedingly dirty, the sidewalks are filled with a motley assortment of cheap wares and edibles, and the entire locality is buzzing with Chinamen, of all degrees, who go clattering along in their uncomfortable, ungainly shoes, with pig-tail flying, and gesticulating and vociferating in their strange unearthly lingo. It certainly does not possess an attractive outlook, yet the woman who visits this city and does not spend three-fourths of her time, and all her money, in this locality is indeed an anomaly.

Inside, the stores are neat, and goods are tastefully arranged. The attendants are all of the shaven-head pig-tail variety. Nearly all speak English, as much as has commercial value, and the celerity with which they reckon an account is indeed marvellous. To attempt a description of what they have for sale would be worse than useless. From the finest crape goods, embroidered and plain, the most delicate Satsuma and valuable Cloisonné, the wonderful carved ivories and transparent tortoise shell, many-hued silk embroideries, fans, paper knives, canes, and screens, to the veriest trash—it is all there ready to be disposed of, at such price as will ensure them a fair profit. As salesmen they are most indifferent, carrying on a conversation of apparently great moment among themselves while you are striving to obtain a price. They will hesitate and often refuse to get goods out without you promise to purchase, and I really think that next to seizing his queue the greatest offense you can commit is to remove a crape shawl from the box, where it is folded with a degree of precision they claim not to be able to repeat. Sometimes they will abate a trifle in price, but generally stick to the figures first named, and no amount of bickering or sham attempts to leave the store will cause the slightest deviation from the rule. The risk is not on their side, so well are they persuaded that the influx of visitors is never ending, and each day increases the stock of new and verdant patrons. Some of the table covers, portières and screens are the most marvellous specimens of handiwork, but their hues are loud and the fabric on which they are wrought of poor quality.

You do not see your friends at your hotel, but you are sure to meet them in Chinatown. No one was ever known to be too ill to climb the hill leading thereto, at least once each day.

Besides these shops for the display and sale of bric-a-brac there are markets, grocery stores and clothing establishments, for there is a resident population of thirty thousand, whose appetites are to be catered to, and bodies clothed in their unseemly style. Much of their food is dried. Oysters, fish, ducks, pork, and things of a kindred nature, are dried and pressed while raw, and then after being exposed to wind, dust and sun for an indefinite time, they are ready, without further preparation, for the table. Their vegetables are mostly a coarse-leafed dock, onions, garlic, turnips, artichokes, with an occasional bunch of lettuce. The climate here renders it possible both summer and winter to carry on this traffic in rooms which are entirely open to the street, with a liberal supply of barrels of fish, casks containing pickles, and potatoes ad infinitum piled almost over the entire sidewalk. There are men, a few women and multitudinous boys who brush against you, clattering their shoes, chattering, driving bargains, and apparently the busiest people in this town of many industries.

Is my picture so attractive as to make you wonder why we all flock hither? I promise you it is not overdrawn. At night the scene shifts, and it would indeed be a valorous heart who would go into the inner courts of this strange, wicked spot without the guardianship of the law. One visit, however, will suffice. It is an experience which will last a lifetime. The party generally consists of not more than eight persons and the guide. At eight p. m.

you sally forth. The horrors of the place have been so often, and with so much latitude, described that you scarce know what to expect, and are ready for murder, arson, gambling, opium smoking, and robbery. *Your* catalogue contains almost every form of vice, and with beating heart you await it. There may be depths lower than those to which we sank. It was simply a disgusting sight, free from the least suspicion of crime or violence. My feeling was pity and disgust, not horror.

Our first visit was to the drug-store, where we watched them compounding a twenty-five-cent prescription. The ingredients were dried caterpillars, roaches, a small lizard, some sassafras bark, a trifle of tansy, a little elecampane, and other roots and herbs unknown to us. These "simples" were warranted to relieve sore throats, weak eyes, dyspepsia, and cuts or bruises. A very fine tea, which was said to be a specific remedy for headache, could be made by boiling the first two articles on the list. The clerks seemed quite capable, and handled their diminutive scales with knowledge and precision. All their remedies are of a similar character, and are said to possess wonderful powers of healing.

We next climbed up the steep steps to the joss house, or church. There are several, but this is the finest. Everywhere there seem to be degrees in religion, at least in its outward observances. Here we found quite pretentious rooms, with handsomely carved wooden altars, elaborately embroidered hangings and panels, and teak-wood tables and chairs delicately inlaid with pearl. We saw, but were not allowed to approach, their deity and a good devil, both of whom are kept in good spirits by liberal offerings of cooked food and libations of whisky, which invariably disappear after service. A medium-sized furnace, where all small articles belonging to deceased members are incinerated, stands in a convenient corner; and a band of musicians, with horns, anvils, cymbals, and indescribable instruments, keep up for hours a species of shrill, horrible sounds, considered by them a form of religious worship. There was a strange incongruity in their performance, seemingly opposed to anything like a religious exercise. But why cavil? They were apparently sincere and we presume a law unto themselves.

We next inspected a jewelry establishment, saw curious rings, daggers for the hair, ear-rings, and other ornaments, all made with cunning and beauty, and an attention to nicety of detail not always observed in modern manufactories. The mode of throwing light upon their work was an original one, and the tools used were of the rudest and most primitive pattern.

Carefully picking our way down two pairs of rickety stairs, our only light a single taper in the hand of our guide, we found ourselves in a narrow subterranean passage or tunnel which led to the lodging-houses of this homeless race. I had no idea of the number around us; they seemed to grow and multiply, and all showed the same pictures of abject misery. The atmosphere was thick with smoke and heavy with the fumes of opium. There was not a breath of fresh air or chance for ventilation, yet here these people live year after year, in some instances with only an occasional glimpse of the outer world. Their beds are simply shelves, without a vestige of mattress, with a little bench which serves as a pillow. Cover they need not, since they seldom remove any garments. Beside them is a small lamp in the flame of which they cook the opium, and then introducing it into a large, unwieldy pipe, smoke until every sensibility is deadened; and, debauched and stupefied, they sink into oblivion. They are generally shoeless, and lie crouched in a most uncomfortable position, the opium jar and knife near at hand, their only desire forgetfulness. Some of them stared at us with a stony glare; by others we were unnoticed. One man over eighty years old was said not to have left his bed for three years, yet he smoked with uncommon energy and eagerly grasped the dime which the guide threw toward him. We saw hundreds of men all in the same position, but in different stages of stupefaction; and I wonder that some awful pestilence does not overtake them and blot them from the earth. There was a horrible smell of decayed fish, unclean animal matter, refuse, and kerosene oil. Altogether it is a most revolting sight. In some of the rooms they were gambling by means of checkers, and the low cunning displayed on their countenances and the avidity with which they caught up their winnings showed what a great hold this dreadful vice has upon them. The police have descended upon some of the worst of these "hells," and fear of punishment will for the time make them cautious. Gambling amounts to a passion with all classes. They will work hard all day, and at night risk at a game of chance all they have made. The taper which our guide held would frequently be extinguished or else burn but dimly in the thick and murky atmosphere. A few sickly kerosene lamps lighted the dens. I only wonder visitors do not break their necks groping around. However, the foul air and fumes of the pipes serve to make them beat a hasty retreat and leave the poor, miserable creatures to the maudlin life they so dearly love.

Here is a field for missionary labor. No need to send to Africa when within a stone's throw of civilization and the refinements of life can be found this class of degraded human beings. Do I think the outlook encouraging for that sort of labor? No. Hercules, when he attempted to cleanse the Augean stables, had a slight task compared to this.

Above this subterranean horror we found the theatre packed, every seat and aisle, with men and boys. Strange as it may seem, women are not allowed to sit in public with the other sex; it is not considered decorous; so they occupy the gallery, accompanied in many instances by their children. They are bare-headed, carry fans, and frequently smoke cigarettes. Admission by the front door was impossible, so we passed through the dressing-rooms, where the players, all men, were in the different stages of attiring and making up their characters. There is no scenery, and but few stage properties. When a sword was required one was brought in, the chairs were arranged in any necessary position, and every surrounding advanced in full view of the audience as the play progressed. The orchestra, which produced a series of most discordant and unearthly sounds, occupied the back part of the stage, and the members smoked their pipes and exchanged greetings with different persons who entered. Camp-stools were provided for us, and we seemed part yet not of the performance. There was a constant disturbance, in which the ubiquitous small boy played a conspicuous part, a universal moving to and fro of all concerned, and a general air of disquiet pervaded the whole place. The play is apparently interminable, commencing at six p. m. and continuing until midnight each night. It is in the style of a serial story, and frequently lasts a month. There was a great deal of gesticulation, some melodramatic situations, and what appeared to be a witty dialogue. The plot embraced cutting off a man's head, the punishment of the murderer, and the subsequent grief of the widow. Of course there was a learned judge, who stroked continuously a patriarchal beard. The head, which had been severed, was offered in evidence, and the widow, a highly-painted piece of ceramics, spoke her lines in a high falsetto voice. The culprit was evidently a droll sort of fellow, for the audience broke into shouts of laughter whenever he appeared.

To us the performance was crude and unsatisfactory and most unreal, and we looked upon it with the same degree of disgust as they would manifest if forced to endure an intensely fashionable operatic performance with us. It really was a remarkable scene—the dusky faces of the audience, their willingness to be amused, the perfect familiarity between actor and listener, and above all the very matter-of-fact way in which people, costumes and stage paraphernalia made their entrance and exit. Nearly all the men who were not smoking were chewing sugarcane, and a variety of sweets was offered for sale.

It being nearly midnight we adjourned to a neighboring restaurant, a place more civilized than anything we had seen. In a room handsomely ornamented with wood-carvings, and papered and frescoed in modern style, we sat upon teak-wood chairs and sipped from tiny cups the genuine Bohea. It was fragrant and delightful. Each bowl contained the leaves, upon which boiling water was poured and allowed to stand a couple of minutes before using. The accompaniments to this cup which "cheers but not inebriates" were very good preserved ginger, limes, and a peculiar sweet, sticky nut. The tea they claim is the best that can be bought, and is retailed at three dollars a pound.

Very few of the Chinese can speak English, save that which serves them in a commercial manner. There generally is one in each establishment who understands tolerably well, and he acts as interpreter. As accountants they are wonderful and will make you a correct bill with neatness and great celerity. They have a system of wooden knobs by which they reckon, useful to them but entirely unintelligible to us. Ask them a question, they smile, give a blank nod, and say nothing; but attempt to trifle with their goods or prices, and they become voluble—quite equal to the occasion.

There are said to be thirty thousand men and eight hundred women in this city. Many of them are frugal and thrifty; but the money once earned, if not gambled away, goes back to China. Their capacities as servants are good; they work early and late, and are strong, capable and willing. Their vices are many, and such as unfit them to dwell in your homes or obtain your confidence.

Our dark night's experience was not entirely satisfactory; we had heard so much of these midnight horrors we expected to see what was really bad, or at least vicious. We expected vice, and were disappointed that we found only depravity. Of the stench of the opium dens no one can form an adequate idea, but the poor, unfortunate slave whom we found there, bound hand, foot and soul to an unrelenting master, deserved our pity as well as condemnation.

When the morning dawned, and Nature put on her pleasant sunny smile, I rubbed my eyes and wondered if the adventures of the previous night were not a dream. For if such things be, woe to the future of this city! Vice, unrebuked, takes no backward step. These people have a religion, but it appears not to be a restraining one. Our guide told us that no matter how bad the haunt or nefarious the business, there was always a joss to whom they offered homage and endeavored to propitiate, evidently thinking, with the Dean of Christchurch, that "Religion not only ensures us salvation in the next world, but also leads to honors and emoluments in this."

X.

MONTEREY.

Hotel del Monte—A Drive by the Sea—San José—Mount Hamilton—Lick Observatory and Its Founder.

It seemed fitting after the noise and bustle of the great, wide-awake city of San Francisco that we should seek the quiet of Monterey, and amid the beauty, seclusion and sylvan loveliness of Hotel del Monte once more enjoy Nature in her fairest mood. Fortunately for us, the autumnal rains had ceased when we reached California in November, and as we revelled in the benefits thereof we rather enjoyed the speculations which we heard in regard to the much-needed rain-fall of the early spring. For months the sky was cloudless, and as blue as Italy. Some of the timorous made grave predictions in regard to the smallness of the crops. The roads were frightfully dusty, and everything seemed parched and thirsty. After a few premonitory clouds the windows of heaven were opened, and for fourteen consecutive days and nights the deluge descended.

Had it continued much longer gopher-wood must have been in demand, and an ark our only means of safety. It was unceasing but satisfactory. Each day the papers announced the amount which had fallen. It was computed by inches, telegrams were sent from obscure stations to say it was "still raining," and from the pulpits the Lord was complimented on the capital way He attended to His works. The whole country was not only moist but in a ferment, and we visitors from the land of perpetual storms looked in wonder at the commotion. What mattered it that bridges and railways were swept away, that telegraph and postal communication ceased, that the gold-diggings were flooded and the disappointed miners starving; the glad tidings came that the crops were safe. Once more the sun shone and the people rejoiced. Destined to be the greatest agricultural and fruit-raising state in the Union, California suffers from insufficient irrigation and lack of rain, and every thinking person must see the great amount of capital jeopardized by a drought, and be thankful when the much-needed storm descends. Still, I was not prepared for quite so much of it. The dose was a regular old-fashioned allopathic one.

Hotel del Monte, in its fine grove of cedar, oak and pine, the loveliest spot on our continent, is garden-like in appearance and park-like in extent. Never but once have I seen its beauty equalled, and then at Chatsworth, the world-famous home of the Duke of Devonshire. There are nearly two hundred acres under cultivation, and upon them is employed a force of sixty men, who keep the flower-beds, walks and turf in the highest state of order and perfection. Flowers in exquisite designs meet you at every turn, and all a mass of harmonizing yet contrasting colors. Great trees, whose bare trunks are entwined with ivy, sweet pea, wisteria, nasturtium and cobæa, raise their proud heads and bid defiance to the storm. The turf is like velvet in texture and emerald in hue. Myriads of roses, unnumbered varieties of clematis, tulips, hyacinths, narcissus, laurestinas, callas, stock-gillies, rich-hued wall-flowers, gay flaunting scarlet poppies, orange-colored calendulas and pansies, with their quaint, pert faces, and a hundred other varieties, delight the eye and make the air fragrant. To walk in the early morning is like a dream of fairy-land. A million dew-drops sparkle in the sun-light. The sky is like that of Sorrento, the birds sing their first and sweetest notes, and nature seems awake and chanting the praises of her Maker. A lake, whose limpid waters reflect the tropical foliage which surrounds it, is one of the features of the place, while fountains, swings, croquet grounds, tennis courts and bowling-alleys are provided in this leafy bower for the entertainment of the guests. Then over and above all is the roar and beat of the grand old ocean, which surges and swells by day and night, and knows no governing power save that of the Creator. On the hotel itself too much praise cannot be bestowed. It is a model of neatness and excellence, the fit accompaniment of its beautiful setting.

The one great feature of the place is a drive of seventeen miles, partly by the sea, over cliff and rock, and returning through a bosky dell. Here the "breaking waves dash high," and it is indeed "on a stern and rock-bound coast." The gentle Pacific belies her name and sets at defiance her traditions, for the great waves rush in mad fury fifty feet high, then break and scatter, reflecting in the sun-light their splendor, making a hundred rainbows ere they reach the sandy beach. Down the long line of ages has this wondrous spectacle been each day repeating its magnificence, and to the end of time will be heard the song of its wonder and greatness. In its incursions the sea has indented the shore with promontories, and here upon the rocks the fishermen climb to secure shells, mosses and sea-weeds, and thus eke out a scanty livelihood. One of the curiosities is to watch the seals climb upon the rocks, and with their hoarse, savage bark seem to invite your attention. What ugly, ungainly creatures they are, but how dexterously they slip about, now quarreling, then embracing, and finally leaping back to their watery home. A few Chinese, about the only people you see, earn a precarious existence by securing the Abilone shells, which, after extracting the contents for food, they polish and offer for sale to the many visitors. The condition of these people is beyond description. Their homes or huts are worse than pens. They are filthy in their personal habits and surroundings, yet they raise large families of sleek and apparently healthy children; while as regards preservation, the parents are models of strength and activity. It is inconsistent that any race should thrive amid so much dirt; yet they do, and volumes may be written in regard to hygiene and nutrition, which will not produce similar results.

There are a few other drives in country highways, and of course a Mission, but visitors will find little outside the grounds to interest them.

The town of Monterey is inconsiderable in size and forlorn in appearance. The old adobe house, where General Fremont first hoisted the American flag, still stands, in a dilapidated condition. In the adjacent village of Pacific Grove a large number of people congregate during the summer months, and live in tents or small frame cottages. I know of no spot in which natural advantages have been so well supplemented by man as at Hotel del Monte, and the fiend who lighted the torch which reduced it to ruins a few years ago deserves the severest punishment that can be inflicted. Many of the trees show marks of the fiery conflict to which they were exposed, but the utmost care has been taken to efface these scars; and in rebuilding not only beauty and durability have been considered, but safety, in case of a similar accident or crime.

San José, to which tourists naturally turn, is a thriving city in the charming Santa Clara valley. It is the abode of people of wealth and culture, and is so embowered with flowers as to make it a veritable garden spot. The lilac bushes are masses of graceful blossoms, and the Lady Banksia rose entwines every porch and fence. For miles surrounding the city, and upon the foot-hills, are immense orchards of peach, plum, apple, apricot and cherry, the trees covered with millions of snowy blossoms, forming the most magnificent agricultural bouquet I have ever seen. The whole air was redolent with the spicy smell, and there was promise of a glorious yield of fruit. Here are said to be raised the finest cherries in the world, approaching in size the plums we so much prize, and surpassing in flavor the productions of other sections. Almost every fruit or berry which is mammoth in size, however, gains that excellence at the expense of delicacy and taste.

Crowning Mount Hamilton, some twenty miles distant, stands in bold relief the Lick Observatory, designed to perpetuate the name of the founder and be a monument for the development of scientific research and the diffusion of knowledge among men. Used for astronomical purposes, it is perfectly equipped and surpasses in its appliances any other observatory in the world. Poor old Lick! I wondered as I stood beside his monument and tomb whether he slept as quietly as those in humbler graves. The wind whistled a fierce and continual requiem. The clouds obscured the world around us, and the heavy machinery creaked and groaned as it was displayed. The great pendulum of the astronomical clock beat in slow and measured movements, and the whole place seemed sepulchral and drear. Yet the founder of all lies there in solemn silence, and the world goes on. As a boy and man his cotemporaries describe him as penurious, fretful in disposition, becoming rich not by sagacity but by opportunity. A Pennsylvanian by birth, he lived in many lands, always acquiring property, to which he clung with bull-dog tenacity, until in 1860 he was one of the richest men in the state. Then came his perplexity as to what to do with his millions. A son born out of wedlock bore his name, but as a stigma of disgrace. The father did not desire that he should inherit his fortune. So he made deeds and grants, appointed trustees and revoked their office, transferred some property and retained other, until finally the stern summons came which admitted of no delay, and, poor and unknown as the veriest pauper, he went alone into the great hereafter. In 1876 he died, and was buried in Lone Mount Cemetery. Two years after, his body was exhumed, and like that of Sir Christopher Wren, who was interred in St. Paul's, the monument of his genius, Mr. Lick was brought up the mountain and placed under the many tons of masonry and telescope created by his fortune.

I am firmly convinced that posthumous generosity is of but little account in this world. I do not know how it will stand on the balance-sheet in the next. For a man, with no endearing trait of character, to hold on to vast sums, when he can only use what suffices for food and raiment, until powers of mind and body failing he reluctantly deeds his property to a charity, the workings of which he will never see and the good which he intends seldom realized— that, from my standpoint, is not benevolence. How much better while in the prime of life and usefulness "to do good and forget not"; to be in a measure your own executor, and make the world better because you have lived; to be active in good works, philanthropic in spirit, and an honor to your age and generation.

The ride to Mount Hamilton is one of great picturesque beauty. It is a succession of fertile tracts, fruit orchards and vineyards. Never have I seen such rich loam as the furrow revealed, never have I known such lush grass as those meadow lands produce. Cattle, horses and sheep graze on the hill-side, and wheat, barley and potatoes grow in such luxuriance as to promise immense profit. The clouds hung over the valley, but their silver lining was often apparent. Soon we soared above them, and were presented with a vernal panorama such as I may never see equalled. The whole ride is a succession of beautiful pictures and surprises. There are three hundred and sixty-five turns in the road. The situation intensifies the hue of hill and dale, and, with a gleam of the bay in the distance, we descend over a road as hard as an Alpine pass into the fertile garden of the Santa Clara valley.

California possesses such a variety of features that the visitor may travel months and always find revealed some new delight. Its progress has been something remarkable. In 1847, just forty-two years ago, there was no such thing as a mail. Letters came straggling in by chance ships from China, Callao, and the Sandwich Islands. Official documents which started in September reached Monterey in May. Now one reads in San Francisco on Saturday the paper which is printed in Philadelphia on the Monday previous.

In an exhaustive article in a recent number of the *North American Review*, Gen. W. T. Sherman, one of the pioneers, says: "In forty years California passed through the same phases of civilization which England did in one thousand years. Such transformations have not occurred in the same time since the creation of the earth, and seem more like the fables of Arabian Nights than a reality. Yet these things are the creations of American energy."

XI.

YOSEMITE VALLEY.

The Journey Thereto—Something About This Great Wonder—Personal Mention—The Mariposa Big Trees.

To make successfully the tour of the Yosemite Valley requires nerve, strength and endurance. The way is long, precipitous and stony, but the reward is great. Artists may depict upon canvas, the camera reproduce with faithful minuteness, and the poet describe in words that burn—all efforts fall short in conveying any adequate idea of the grandeur of this greatest wonder of the Creator's hand.

There stand the mighty pillars of stone as they have stood for ages. There fall the majestic cataracts which have surged and beat since the world began, and poor, finite humanity can only come to the brink and gaze with humid eyes at the overpowering scene. I care not whether it sprung into being in one day, or that a thousand years were reckoned as yesterday in the sight of the Creator, it is the most awe-inspiring exhibition of Nature's works the world can produce.

The name Yosemite signifies a great or grizzly bear. Previous to 1851 the valley was the abode of Indians. At that date there were two horseback trails leading to it, and a band of United States troops, to avenge some real or fancied wrong, descended upon the inhabitants and took possession. Dr. Bunnell, who accompanied the expedition, thus writes: "None but those who have visited this most wonderful valley can even imagine the feelings with which I looked upon the view there presented. The grandeur of the scene was but softened by the haze that hung over the valley—light as gossamer—and by the clouds which partially dimmed the higher cliffs and mountains. The obscurity of vision but increased the awe with which I beheld it, and as I looked a peculiarly exalted sensation seemed to fill my whole being, and I found my eyes in tears of emotion."

The valley proper is about eight miles long and one mile wide. It is encircled by a perpendicular wall in some places nine thousand feet above the level of the sea. Prof. J. D. Whitney advances the theory that the bottom of the valley sunk down to an unknown depth owing to its support being withdrawn from beneath. The greatest scientists of modern times have visited and explored the region, and all are lost in wonder at its might, and can only conjecture regarding its age and formation. The soil is of a light gravelly nature, unproductive in its character and easily affected by the weather. An effort has been made during the past few years to introduce fruit trees, but with indifferent success. The forest trees, which are abundant but not of uncommon size, are mostly black and live-oak, a variety of arbor vitæ, maple, dogwood, willow, tamarack, and Douglass spruce. This last is what is otherwise known as Oregon pine, and is the most valuable lumber which can be obtained for building purposes, being almost impervious to water, not affected by climate, and universally used for piles, flumes and trenches.

The journey proper of the valley is embraced in seven days. No heavy baggage is allowed, but good stout shoes and warm clothing are a necessity. By leaving San Francisco in the evening you reach Raymond in the early dawn, and are ready for the ride of sixty miles, two days in duration. At first the way is comparatively pleasant. There are said to be three hundred varieties of flower, shrub and tree in that first day's journey. There are entire fields of lupins, poppies, and the most delicate blue and golden tints. The sun's rays are sufficiently warm but not oppressive. The road is at times rocky, but never of the perilous nature we had heard described. It is steep and rough, the horses feel the loads they draw, but with a fresh relay every six miles you feel that their task is not burdensome; still, while it destroys the romantic aspect, it will be a humanitarian who introduces the iron steed. I do not say this is not a dangerous journey. Accidents do occur, but with stout, sure-footed horses, strong harness, and careful drivers, the risks are not very great. Your sense of enjoyment is so great that all feeling of personal discomfort is forgotten. It is the only scene which far exceeds all expectations. You pass through miles of magnificent specimens of pine trees, many of them measuring fifty feet in circumference, and being one hundred and fifty feet high. These are not occasional instances I am citing. We saw during the journey thousands of that size, well preserved, healthy, and as straight as an arrow. In some localities immense boulders are piled up, then you cross a rippling stream, and anon the mountain torrent dashes down hundreds of feet. There was a sprinkling of snow on the ground, the rain which overtook us in the valley shedding a mantle of white over the peaks and fringing the boughs of the pines with a robe of ermine. The ground is free from underbrush. There is naught to offend the eye, and a sweet, fragrant, woody smell greets the senses. I want my readers to feel that I am giving them no fancy sketch, or depicting things in a roseate light. I am trying to show a plain statement of facts.

The weather this season was exceptional, the roads being open at least a month earlier than usual, and the valley remarkably free from snow. Our greatest foe was mud, and the speed with which we at times descended the mountain was such as to make preservation our first duty, scenery and comfort being for the time ignored.

At noon of the second day you reach Inspiration Point, and the valley in its grandeur lies before you. There stands El Capitan, hoary with the frost of time, the noblest of them all, the undisputed chief among giants, from his cloud-topped head looking down seven thousand feet. You hear the rush of waters, and see the soft-falling, swaying foam, which bounds and meanders a thousand feet in the air before it strikes the rocks and forms the Bridal Veil. The Three Brothers gaze in defiant might, and North Dome looks its almost sculptured beauty, while Clouds' Rest, true to its name and purpose, completes the picture. Meandering peacefully along, as though not cognizant of its place in the book of the world's wonders, flows the Merced river, in its bosom reflecting the majesty of its surroundings.

It is a moment when your strongest and deepest emotions are stirred. It is sublime. Far from the world and men, here, annually, in storm and sunshine, Nature repeats the wondrous tale, and unmoved by the elements, the same yesterday, to-day and forever, is sung the story of the might of the Creator. It has been my lot to wander in many lands, and see the glorious places which men call wonderful; never have I looked upon a sight so inspiring, so majestic, so perfectly incomparable, as the first view of Yosemite.

The descent to the floor of the valley is easy and rapid. For three days we sat at Nature's shrine and learned anew the lesson of her greatness. There are several trails. We chose the one to Glacier Point, eight thousand feet above sea level, and that one experience will suffice. Let no one be discouraged or deterred by reports of dangers to be feared. Every precaution consistent with safety is taken. The road is precipitous, but it is three and sometimes four feet wide, with angles and turns of surprising sharpness, but generally protected by stones, logs or masonry, and in many places made less fearful by a thick growth of under-brush. The horse on which I rode —I use the term entirely by courtesy, for that day I was the creature of circumstance, with neither power nor volition—was quiet, well trained, and with a decided will of his own. Under no form of inducement would he move save in the footsteps of his predecessor. He early showed dissatisfaction with the weight of his load, and gave vent to a series of groans that were not tranquilizing. He also manifested a desire to go perilously near the precipice, and would rest apparently on nothing and at improper occasions.

The view is grand, but appalling. Deep down in the mountain-walled gorge before us sleeps the valley; its beautiful glades, its peacefully glinting river, its dark green pines, its heavily timbered slopes, all hemmed in by cliff-encompassing domes. No change of time or circumstance can ever efface from memory this ride to Glacier Point. One misstep, a falling rock, and there could be no salvation. You have taken, as it were, your life in your hands.

When near the summit our path ran between snow drifts from four to six feet high. These banks were rapidly melting, augmenting the bodies of water which compose the different falls, and making the trails moist and slippery. The only shrub you see is a dwarf live-oak, manzanitas, and a few chinquapin bushes. The manzanita, with its pinkish white, wax-like and globe-shaped blossoms hanging in bunches, challenges our admiration. Save for beauty, these specimens are of but little use. The wood when young is soft, and is easily borne down and made crooked by the weight of the snow. That which grows upon the river bank is tall, lithe and straight, susceptible of a high polish when used for canes and ornamental purposes.

For four and a half miles we trudged this weary way; and then, when the summit was gained, we suffered disappointment, for the clouds which had hung at our feet all day long developed into a thick mist and completely hid the glories we had climbed so far to see. Encouraged by the custodian we waited, but only to see it become more and more impenetrable, and with beating, quaking hearts we took up the march for our descent.

Of the details of the return journey I am not sufficiently composed to write in a disinterested manner. The view is still there, each turn was made with precision, but the relief with which the base was reached told the tale of fear and suffering. When next I visit Glacier Point the trail will lead me to the summit, but the stage, four horses and a cautious driver will carry me from that eminence to Clark's. This little piece of information I gained, and will bestow upon those who follow me over that beaten but perilous track. Once and only once before had I seen my spouse under similar trying circumstances—then a score of years ago, when we bestrode what the people of Killarney facetiously termed "ponies." Time has robbed his figure of the grace of youth and added to his avoirdupois, still the agility with which he mounted and the determination with which he avoided looking at what he came to see, made an indelible impression upon my mind, and I determined that as our horsemanship was only intended for show places, this, our second, should be our last appearance. Henceforth those sights which cannot be reached by carriage or on foot will be forever unseen and unregretted by us. Truthfully has Starr King written, "Nowhere among the Alps, in no pass of the Andes, and in no canyon of the mighty Oregon range, is there such stupendous rock scenery as the traveler here lifts his eye to." There is on every side an overpowering sense of the sublime. It is the crowning glory of all views. We are shut in by mountain walls, only three thousand feet we say, but so immense is everything that figures have lost their meaning, and everything is swallowed up and obliterated by the immeasureable stony heights that look down upon us. You could spend months viewing this scenic beauty, the memory of which is like the mercies of the Almighty, "new every morning and fresh every evening."

It seems almost presumptuous for me to attempt a description of what the greatest minds of the century have acknowledged their inability to depict. The longer we gaze, the greater is our wonder. And in ending this imperfect sketch we might quote the words of James Vick, who gave as his impression that "the road to Yosemite, like the way of life, is narrow and difficult, but the end, like the end of a well spent life, is glorious beyond the highest anticipations."

It was our very good fortune while in the valley to meet Mr. Galen Clark, a man who is an enthusiast in regard to its beauties, a compendium of knowledge concerning the different localities, and high and reliable authority in relation to formations and statistics. A New Hampshire man by birth and education, Mr. Clark was forced by ill health to seek the mild climate of this section. A love of adventure made him one of the first explorers, and for fourteen years he filled the responsible position of Guardian of the place. His love for the spot is genuine, his pride in it real, and with an interest which none can mistake he leads the visitor where everything appears in its best and noblest aspect. Under his guidance we looked upon Mirror Lake, and saw reflected therein the sun and its innumerable rays; marked the fanciful loveliness of Clouds' Rest when mirrored upon its bosom; drove where Yosemite dashes in broken and triple beauty for three thousand feet; and anon stood and listened with rapt attention to the sounds, which came like artillery, from the Bridal Veil when surged and dashed about by the roaring wind. For ten miles we followed the Merced river, amid rock and tree, until Cascade Fall was reached; then listened as the old man told in tender accents the story of the one dweller in that region who, broken-hearted by the infidelity of one he trusted, crept back to his dishonored hearthstone, and was shot upon the threshold. The home he so fondly reared is now falling to decay. Many of the theories in regard to the glacial period, a prehistoric race, and kindred topics, Mr. Clark has imbibed from the conversation of learned visitors; but his own ideas are original, and he will give you with an uncommon degree of accuracy the time and cause of the falling of fragments, their weight, the devastation wrought by wind and flood, and convey to you in such unmistakable terms his fondness for the place that it is a pleasure to listen to the recital.

Mr. Thomas Hill, an artist of wide repute, whose studio at Wawona attracts many visitors, is also an enthusiast in regard to the charms of the Valley, and has transferred to canvas many phases of the remarkable spot. First, you may look, by means of his brush, from Inspiration Point, or see the scene when every peak is illumined by the setting sun. Again, you may stand and gaze with wondering eyes at the noble fall of water, or from beneath look up to the dome reaching almost to the heavens.

A visit to the remarkable group of big trees at Mariposa Grove concluded the experiences of this memorable week in April. Situated on the top of the mountain, they number six hundred—"the noble six hundred," they may well be called. They are a variety known as Sequoia Gigantea, and partake of the nature of red-wood and cedar. I saw them ninety-nine or thirty-three yards in circumference, and sat in the stage drawn by four horses through one which only measures eighty-four feet. They are from one hundred and fifty to two hundred feet high, and show from their concentric rings or layers that they are over four thousand years old. The bark is soft and spongy and easily detached. The greatest devastation has been done by fire, and nearly every one is partially burned or disfigured. We asked regarding the prevalence of the destroying element, and were told that the herders, to rid the ground of pine needles, which are destructive to vegetation, start forest fires. These trees being old are highly inflammable, and, as a consequence, suffer therefrom. Since the grove has been the property of the state the most stringent regulations are observed, but, unfortunately, too late to prevent the wanton destruction of what may truly be termed a "wonder of the world."

XII.

HOMEWARD.

Mountain Scenery—Salt Lake—Mormonism—Across the Continent—Home Again.

A person who has been on a sight-seeing tour of nearly six months is not likely when on the home-stretch either to stop frequently or to observe any but objects of the greatest interest. The route chosen for our return from California embraced the finest mountain scenery on our continent, and for extent and grandeur is unsurpassed in the world. Crossing in succession the Sierra Nevada, Wahsatch, Rocky and Allegheny mountains, one is treated to such an endless variety of peak, dome, rocky and sandy embankment, that the mind is bewildered by the constant and apparently endless succession. At this season the Denver and Rio Grande claims a large amount of patronage. The road is narrow gauge from Ogden to Denver.

Salt Lake City, the home of the Latter-Day Saints, more than any other town, seems to demand a visit.

Situated on the shores of the great lake from which it derives its name, it is a city of cottage homes and some imposing residences. The streets are broad, not paved, and consequently dirty and extremely dusty. In front of the dwellings are planted double rows of Balm of Gilead, and these, with a profusion of fruit trees and numerous flower gardens, conspire to make the place externally attractive.

It was not, however, the ideal spot I expected to see. There was comfort but a lack of order, and no uniformity but a great deal of original architecture. Z. C. M. I. (Zion's Co-operative Mercantile Institution) seems to monopolize the greater and better part of the business interests, and all engaged under these symbolic letters are followers of the faithful, who give a tithe of their earnings or profits to the church. Since the vigorous opposition and prosecution of polygamy by the United States government the institution no longer flourishes openly, although grave doubts are expressed as to whether the leaders have relinquished their abominable practices. Ephraim is joined to his idols, but he is not let alone, and men prominent in church and society served terms in the penitentiary. An eye-witness told me of many affecting scenes which occurred during these trials. An opportunity was always offered the offenders, when aged and well known, to have their sentences mitigated in case they would promise to live with but one wife, and she the first; but in every case was the clemency of the court refused. The prisoner went to jail and came out a hero, openly living with none to whom he had been sealed. Like his Gentile brother, the Mormon generally selects as his second venture something young, attractive and giddy; and when told that he could have but one, he ignored the claims of the mother of his children and proposed to cling to youth and beauty. Can any one imagine a state of society more heinous, and then to claim that it was sanctioned by God? It is said that the younger members of the society abjure the doctrine of the plurality of wives, which formerly all practiced.

I heard a sad tale of the marital woes of a young couple of wealth, intelligence and refinement. They had been attached to each other for years, and had plighted their vows with the firm understanding that they were to be all the world to each other, "so long as ye both may live." Alas! for the constancy of man. The night his first child was born he brought home and installed another wife. Outraged and infuriated, as soon as possible the poor, forsaken creature took her child and sought the protection of her father, a wealthy banker, but only to be driven from there and told that she was the result of a polygamous marriage, that the institution was recognized by the church, and that she must abide by the consequences. What alternative had she but to return, take up what may well be called the burden of life, and as

> "Heaven has no rage like love to hatred turned,
> Nor hell a fury like a woman scorned,"

the scene may, to use an old-fashioned yet expressive phrase, better be imagined than described.

Old Brigham Young, saint and sinner that he was, sleeps in a pleasant spot on the hill-side. An immense slab of marble covers him, and for a year an armed sentry kept guard lest some one should molest his sacred remains. Around him are five wives, and the returns not all yet in. Amelia, the favorite, lives with her children in what is termed her palace, and the other thirteen are scattered in various directions. The streets swarm with children, objects of our most sincere pity, since on their innocent heads will fall the burden of their parents' transgressions. Still, on every side they are erecting handsome and commodious school houses, and with education, the law and a correct public sentiment, the iniquitous practice may languish, and finally die out. The members deny that two families occupy one house, but from the peculiar external structure, and the almost universal prevalence of two and sometimes three front doors, I prefer to be guided by my judgment rather than believe in their traditions.

The incompleted Temple is a magnificent structure of granite. It is designed to be a monument of the greatness of the church, and is worthy to be compared with the finest specimens of architecture of the Old World. The workmen are engaged upon it during the summer months, and vast piles of material in the rude and dressed state encumber the ground. Superstition prevents its completion, since a prophet of the faith has said that it, like the temple of Jerusalem, will be reared only to be destroyed.

The Tabernacle is an unpretentious building, mammoth in size, without either external or internal decoration. The seats are plain hard wood, the walls white, and the whole lighted by innumerable gas jets. The acoustic properties of the building are something remarkable, and from tests which we witnessed fully justified all that had been said in regard to it. The magnificent organ, the largest in this country, occupies a conspicuous position behind the seats reserved for the Bishops and prominent men. It was our good fortune to be present at a recital on the evening of Good Friday. This mode of entertainment is a new departure in the Mormon Church, and attracted an immense audience of the just as well as the unjust. It is indeed a wonderful instrument, and the vast throng listened with rapt attention to the melody evoked by the organist, assisted by talent, both vocal and instrumental, of the very highest order. The entertainment closed by the singing of the "Hallelujah Chorus," by a choir composed of at least one hundred voices.

I should judge there were six thousand people present, and the utmost decorum was observed. The Cannons, Angus and George, occupied prominent seats, and were active in making announcements, and calling the meeting to order. Bishop Whitney made the opening prayer, and really from his style and fervent petitions I should fail to distinguish him from an orthodox clergyman. He prayed for everything and everybody, especially the stranger from the East, and trusted that all might return home refreshed and benefited by the sight of the love, harmony and industry there exhibited, and closed his exhortation by asking that all mercies be vouchsafed us for the sake of "our dear Redeemer, Thy Son Jesus Christ." The vaulted roof of the building is most elaborately decorated with evergreens and very dilapidated paper flowers. These were put up some five years ago in honor of the visit of Patti, the Queen of Song, and allowed to remain. There really seemed to be an unusual amount of kindly feeling and good fellowship manifested, each one in turn making an address or suggestion, as seemed to suit his fancy. A small pail of water, from which all drank in true democratic style, was freely passed around previous to the exercises. There were several handsome elderly men who made themselves quite conspicuous. We were told that all had been imprisoned for their marital transgressions, but now they lived the lives of good citizens. I saw nothing like the patriarchal families I had been led to expect, and I came to the conclusion that if the vice still flourishes it is conducted *sub rosa*, as in more prominent places.

To the wonderful and fearful beauty of a homeward journey across the continent, who can do justice? Our long train, sometimes drawn by one engine, then by two, wound round the rocky defiles. In the gray of early morning we passed through the Black Canyon, then climbed over Marshall Pass, and in the full effulgence of the noonday sun looked upon the Royal Gorge. Mountains of rocks, running up perpendicularly and terminating in dizzy pinnacles, seem ready to fall on us. Our progress is barred by huge cliffs. The Arkansas river, crowded into narrow limits, seems to dispute the right of way with our snorting steed, and at one spot our foothold is a hanging bridge, the only support of which rests on the opposite wall of the abyss. Awe-inspiring, yet fearful indeed, is that day's ride. At Green river we saw a genuine cowboy and his female prototype, with pistols in belt, gun in hand, and the trophies of the chase at her saddle-bow.

And now, on the morning of the eighth day, how our hearts thrill as we come thundering down the beautiful fertile valleys of the Keystone state. We have crossed the continent but seen nothing so rich as the picture before us. Here thrift, fertility and prosperity walk hand in hand. Here all the good and blessed things of life are surely centered. There are spots where the cloudless sky takes a deeper blue than here, where the elements, instead of resisting, help man's efforts, where seasons come and go with no distinguishing mark. But here, in this valley of content, is our home, and these two simple words fill the measure of perfect happiness. We departed on the most gloomy eve of a dull November day. The skies were leaden, the rain poured, and the wind sang a mournful requiem in the trees. In the glad springtime of another year we return. It is the resurrection of the world, the glorious Easter season, and every blade of grass, each leaf, and innumerable birds sing in glad song their welcome to renewed life and vigor; the sun is glinting every hill-top around the old familiar places, and with heart and mind in tuneful accord we join in the psalm of thanksgiving.

Nature and human nature have both been unrolled before me. I know not which has been the most improving study. I have seen men of the truest type, whose devotion to those about them has renewed my faith in the beautiful chivalry of Sir Philip Sidney, the truest, sweetest type of gentle man. I have seen women whose lives have flowed on in such quiet, pure content, that their souls seemed but mirrors of truth and joy. I have seen vice fairly colonized in San Francisco, and so open in its allurements that the noonday sun brought no blush to those who flaunted their vileness in its rays.

I have lived in the perpetual summer of the tropics, where time and seasons have no existence. The dwellers there have no last spring, no last fall. They have no winter, in which a heavy fall of snow, or the persistent lack of it, has recorded the season as a sort of picture on our memories.

Dear friends and readers, you who have followed me step by step on this journey of many thousand miles, the last chronicle is told, the last picture drawn. I have endeavored to tell faithfully and truthfully of things which interested me, and I trust have not tired you. The trip was one of great pleasure and benefit, marred by no accident, ill health or detention. But I am glad to be with you again—to lay down the pen and to take up the weapons of domestic warfare. Whether the sojourn in sunny lands has benefited me I leave others to judge. Far be it from me to discount the leech's skill, but I have found climate and a good strong will the best physicians, the only true "Christian Science" cure. I have seen much that was good, great and glorious; but no spot so dear as home, no place so grand as to win me from my allegiance. I tried to carry sunshine and a strong determination in my heart. That was half the battle. Sometimes, when in the valley of despondency, I thought of an epitaph penned for me by a friend some years ago. Happily it has never yet been required. But you will all endorse it, for it reads in this wise: "She never neglected an opportunity to enjoy herself."

www.ingramcontent.com/pod-product-compliance
Lightning Source LLC
Chambersburg PA
CBHW030351170426
43202CB00010B/1341